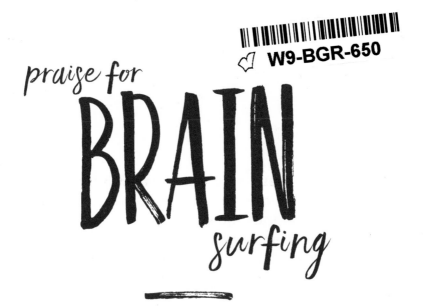

praise for **BRAIN** *surfing*

"**Brain Surfing** is such a delightful book. Not only is it a wonderful journey but, unlike so many other books, it artfully answers the question 'How?' in a delightful and collaborative way. Bravo, Heather!"

John Winsor, Chairman/Founder, Victors & Spoils

"A truly fascinating blend of travel journal and business text, it drifts beautifully between the dreamy rambles of an enthusiastic traveller and the great insights of a business book. *Brain Surfing* should be on every strategist's reading list."

Mark Inskip, CEO, The Futures Company

"On the one hand, you have Heather making us green with envy as she goes to all corners of the globe and gains invaluable experience by talking and spending time with the best brand strategists around the world. On the other hand, you have Heather generously offering the gift of what she learned and her unique point of view. You could call it a fair trade, but that would be an unfair oversimplification. Instead, *Brain Surfing* is a must-read for account planners, brand strategists, and all those who are humble enough to recognize that a lot remains to be unveiled."

Ken Fujioka, Partner and VP of Strategy & Planning at Loducca;
President of the Brazilian Account Planning Group (Grupo de Planejamento)

"If you run a business, a start-up, or a brand, this book is essential reading. Not only did Heather persuade some of advertising's true maverick thinkers to let her stay with them, she also somehow got them to reveal their secret methodologies to how they outthink the competition. Clever."

David Hieatt, Cofounder of Hiut Denim Co and The Do Lectures

"Is strategic ability in the DNA? Is it nature or nurture? Can the kind of problem solving that propels culture and companies forward be taught or is it the stuff of apprenticeship? Heather is just the person to try to unravel this philosophical hairball. Join her on her journey and take advantage of the sharp thinkers she has assembled on these pages."

Caley Cantrell, Head of Communications Strategy Track, Brandcenter/VCU

"Strategists spend so much time applying curiosity and imagination to the lives of brands and consumers. But what happens when you apply that same relentless energy to normal life? That's what this book is about—the strategist's mind, only inverted and directed to the things that actually matter: culture, purpose, humility, family, adventure. Sure, this is required reading for people that want to be strategists, but, more likely, this is required reading for strategists that want to stay people."

Alain Sylvain, Founder, Sylvain Labs

"You'll thoroughly enjoy how Heather has drafted sketches and snapshots that capture the places, smell, culture, and characters so very vividly . . . and then seamlessly brings in some very thought-provoking ideas about what we do for a living— and perhaps more pertinently, how we do it. It's a book about how to rethink, rejuvenate and revitalize our entire industry. In short, it gives me hope."

Bo Hellberg, Executive Creative Director, Edelman

"*Brain Surfing* is *Eat, Pray, Love* for planners, strategists, and people who study brands. The memoir aspects provide a really great context because we get to know the people behind the strategic thinking. Heather has covered a lot of ground and framed today's strategic issues beautifully."

Larry Vincent, Chief Branding Officer, UTA Brand Studio and Author of Brand Real

"Heather has been—in the truest sense—on a lovely journey for a couple of decades. She is the rock flipper, the quirky observer, the curious interviewer; this beautiful approach to life made her a successful planner, an influencer of the craft. What we can learn from her book is that traveling our journey is indeed an act of courage that few of us take. And when she decided to search for herself—seeking something even she couldn't quite describe—she found the stuff of truth and delight. A marvelous philosophy here, the honesty of well-crafted work there, and some bullshit and bravery that compelled her to find her life. All of this makes for a delightful personal journal that should be required reading for the smartest career-driven strategists."

Deborah Morrison, PhD, Chambers Distinguished Professor of Advertising, University of Oregon

"There is no other book on strategy that takes such a broad look; Heather doesn't boil it all down into one tidy flawed model. *Brain Surfing* recognizes the interconnectedness of influences and inspiration that create truly original strategic thinking."

Tom Bassett, Founder of MindSwarms and Bassett & Partners

"It takes someone like a Heather to take a step back, focus on the discipline, and share her learnings. This book will save you a year of research and a trip around the world."

Rikki Khanna, Partner, Khanna \ Reidinga

"During Heather's adventures you see her perceptions on marketing, business, and even her future as a strategist evolve. This is an unexpected business book—the best kind!"

Pippa Seichrist, Co-Founder and Head of Innovation & Development, Miami Ad School

"The only way to truly understand culture is to live it. Heather has created the ultimate ethnography by moving in with the people who watch others for a living. A fascinating blend of travel, observation, and insight."

Tom Sacchi, Founding Partner, UNIT9

"A good strategist is able to bring new perspective to any problem. Heather has traveled the world to seek out new thinking from the brightest minds in marketing. I was as entertained by her stories of living with people in the business as I was fascinated by the insights she gleaned along the way."

Rye Clifton, Experience Director, GSD&M

BRAIN
surfing

THE TOP MARKETING
STRATEGY MINDS IN THE WORLD

HEATHER LeFEVRE

Foreword by Toma Bedolla

Miami, FL

ISBN 978-0-9968546-0-3 (paperback)
ISBN 978-0-9968546-1-0 (ebook)

Editing by Marissa van Uden
Cover and text design by Michael Kinlan
Cover illustration by Michael Kinlan
Interior illustrations by Eroica De Souza
Printed and bound in the United States of America

15 16 17 18 19   5 4 3 2 1

CONTENTS

ACKNOWLEDGMENTS

First and foremost, this book would not have been possible without the spirit of adventure embodied in each of my nine fine coaches. My life has forever been enhanced by all of you. Thank you, Jason Oke, Simon Kemp, rOobin Golestan, Rob Campbell, Phil Adams, Suzanne Powers, Kevin May, Saher Sidhom (who also came up with the brilliant book title), and Brian Millar. I am also grateful for the sage feedback, round after round, with each of you directly. You helped me write a better book.

This compassionate spirit was matched only by each of the families who hosted me. Thank you, Meredith, Millie, Dash and Twyla Oke; Sarah Kemp; Katrin Fremmer; Leo and Henry Golestan; Jill and Otis Campbell; Rachel, Molly, Penny, Lois, and Madeleine Adams; Christine and Charlotte May; Samira Ahmed; and Arun and Lakshmi Millar.

I cannot thank my editor, Marissa van Uden, enough. She's the person who saved my sanity and guided me through my first book. Though she prefers to work with sci-fi and fantasy, I am so grateful Marissa was willing to make one of her few exceptions for *Brain Surfing*. You'll not go wrong talking to her about an editing project, and she can be found at marissavu.com.

To the rest of my book production team, thank you for being excellent in your craft: Michael Kinlan, who designed the cover and interior of the book; Speros Zakas and Ginny Carroll, who proofread; Eroica De Souza, who did the illustrations of each coach and me; Alberto Amóros, who provided legal advice; and Trena White, who gave me structural editing advice at the beginning when all I had was a meandering mess and guided me through the publishing production process.

A few times on my journey, in between staying with my mentors, other friends and acquaintances also let me stay with them or went way out of their way to show me around. Thank you, Argha Sen; Pete Heskett and Melani Finn; Tibor, Arlo, and Bea Heskett; Libby Schaub; Sushobhan Mukherjee; and Katie Johnston.

Writing this book has taught me just how busy we all are these days, and yet so many lovely people offered to beta read draft chapters or made time for me to interview them, and for this I am truly grateful. Thank you, Faris Yakob, Katie Dreke, Heidi Hackemer, Marquis Duncan, Matthew Scott, Rye Clifton, Ashly Stewart, David Martin Johnstone, Bo Hellberg, Frank Amóros, Pete Gagliardi, Toma Bedolla, Mark Inskip, Cameron Maddux, Caley Cantrell, Ivan Askwith, Sudeep Gohil, David Hieatt, Ken Fujioka, Amr Assaid, Tom Sacchi, Tom Bassett, Alain Sylvain, Pippa Seichrist, Rikki Khanna, Richard "Goz" Gostelow, Bartholomew Motes, Deborah Morrison, Dan Mintz, Colleen Murray, Russell Davies, Clay Langdon, Adrian Ho, John Winsor, Gareth Kay, Larry Vincent, Lee Feldman, Matthew Curlewis, Cassandra Rivas, Keith Stoeckeler, Dave McCaughan, Noah Brier, Jason De Turris, Andrew Teagle, and Ann Iverson.

Hyper Island has provided me with the invigorating work all around the world that supported me when I needed the flexibility to finish this book. To all of the incredible people who make Hyper Island what it is and who teach me new things every day, I thank you: Alys Arden, Mark Comerford, Jaclyn Ciamillo, Sky Freyss-Cole, Joelle Panisch, Joakim Jardenberg, Per Håkansson, Anders Sjöstedt, Laura Sawyer, Buz Sawyer, Mathias Jakobsen, Terri Simon, Marcus Collins, Hazel Swayne, Amy Rae, Jonathan Briggs, Sarah Gregersen, Per Vidar Lundberg, Peter Hagander, Nathalie Trutmann, Kristian Kruse, Maria Eriksson, Christina Andersson, Lisa Pertoso, and every last one of the hundreds of masterclass students who I've had the honor to meet.

I am so thankful for the support of my amazing friends and family. Thank you, Heather Sullivan, Sophia Farrag, Vivian Bernstein, Laura "Broodje" van den Boom, Omar Ramirez, Hilary Metcalfe, Mariota Essery, Sean Chambers, Malin Hanås, Sharon Sullivan, Georgette Kolkman, Elizabeth Vaughn, Manuel Mazzanti, Gerald and Lisa Gallagher, Casey Gallagher, and Melinda Eskell.

Finally, when it's all said and done, there's really just one person who I hope is proud of me for this project. He's the guy I met the day before heading to Scotland for the book, the guy who moved to the US to be with me, and who has cheered me up and talked me off the ledge whenever I thought I'd never finish this effing book: thank you to my husband, Aaron De Sturler.

FOREWORD
by toma bedolla

What's interesting about the title of a book is how it captures your attention or curiosity, how it conveys or conceals what's inside. It is my hope that this book's title helps it land in the Surfing section of bookstores rather than Marketing. Please don't get me wrong; there's plenty of marketing genius and nuggets in here, but that's really the last thing you should take away from these pages. What you're holding in your hands or reading on your screen is better described as the story of a creative and courageous woman who has grabbed life by the balls and embarked on a journey that honors the inspiration of an *Eat, Pray, Love* while feeling more like *The Hitchhiker's Guide to the Galaxy* without the towel.

All too often, marketing books are one person's account or theory on their way to approach or disrupt the industry. The next big thing in our endless quest as marketers to stand out from the crowd. We all know the script: Find the lens no one else is looking through to help others see the world and/or a product in an entirely new way. Yet we're all reading the same book.

To reveal and shape perspective is both the gift and responsibility of the marketing community. To do this effectively, one must discover and hold as many possible perspectives or unique lenses as possible, upon which you eventually add your own.

That's what sets this book apart from the norm. In these pages is an experience of putting yourself out there, sometimes way out there, in order to discover the remarkable thinking, places, and people that exist beyond the space between your ears or the zip code you live in. This book is a thought-provoking collection of life lessons, gathered in a highly unconventional manner and turned into marketing insights from a potpourri of great minds . . . the revelations of how they creatively view and hack life.

This book is also like a feline: It's nine lives (or books) in one. Except that after reading, it's highly unlikely that any two people will apply these lessons or ideas in the same manner. It's a perfect launchpad—symbolically, creative rocket fuel for the mind.

It occurred to me as I read the book for the first time that Heather was not just good people, she was one of my own tribe. Accused of going "where the wind takes me" and hopping from one adventure to the next, I've been fortunate to experience enough stories worth sharing to be good company for at least one evening of food and wine. Maybe. Heather has upped the stakes. Since we met a few years ago, when she helped me expand an organization I co-founded into Amsterdam, she's been busy getting married, moving internationally, performing her first ever stand-up comedy at an Improv, becoming certified as a multidimensional trainer in yoga, and I think also visiting the space station or something while somehow finding time to write this book.

Every bit as brilliant and impressive as the people she's chased down in this adventure, Heather's best quality by far is her willingness to laugh at herself, which is why I think she's so good at holding true to herself no matter how foreign or uncomfortable the situation. This affords her the chance to absorb new and often unorthodox perspectives that she then applies to her craft, which is arguably as much business and problem solving as it is marketing. She writes like she speaks, so when you read this, you'll be getting to know one of the most impressive women you'll ever meet in all walks of life.

Toma Bedolla, CEO & Co-Founder House of Genius
Adventurously spirited, physics minded, entrepreneurial madman
with a bent toward technology and hanging out with fellow brain surfers

INTRODUCTION

I once read Mitch Albom's *Tuesdays with Morrie* (don't judge) and felt compelled to copy the ending into my notebook:

> *Have you ever really had a teacher? One who saw you as a raw but precious thing, a jewel that, with wisdom, could be polished to a proud shine? If you are lucky enough to find your way to such teachers, you will always find your way back.*

In my experience, only if you are very lucky will someone take enough interest to dedicate his or her time to teach you. Instead, usually you have to find ways to be satisfied with merely observing the leaders in the companies where you work or with reading the online musings of the practitioners generous enough to share their insights. That's how it's been for me, anyway, in most of my fourteen years as a strategist.

Lots of people have "strategist" or "strategic" in their title, but I'd bet money a good majority of them are 100 percent adults doing grown-up work in pleated slacks. I, on the other hand, have the ultimate Peter Pan type job where I get paid to play with ideas. In the world of advertising agencies where I've worked, my career has proved to be almost a calling.

While I began my career working for respected integrated shops in the US (Mullen, The Martin Agency and Crispin Porter + Bogusky), it wasn't until I moved to the Netherlands that I got to try my hand at international business and digitally led ideas at Tribal DDB and StrawberryFrog.

As my resume got longer, my strategy skills grew and became applicable to more and more roles. In addition, the changing business landscape opened opportunities for me to focus on a proliferation of possible specialties: for example, digital, social, channel, or user-experience strategy. The types of companies hiring strategists snowballed beyond agencies to include innovation consultancies, start-ups, and even the marketing departments on the client side. As my brain grappled with this paradox of choice, my own insecurity would nag, *Why don't I feel like an expert yet? What don't I know that I need to learn?*

Advertising agencies have all but abandoned training programs—not so smart in a business that depends on people's performance. As an employee with various agencies, I've been sent to the occasional conference or three-day presentation skills seminar, but I've never been presented with a company curriculum designed with the objective of developing my skills. This has frustrated me and, at times, made me feel like I'm just trading my time on this planet for a paycheck. I want more.

My past assumptions about how to gain expertise had led me to believe that excellence requires a convergence of innate abilities, motivation, and learning the right skills (not to mention a bit of luck).

I thought I had a good amount of intense practice at learning the right skills under my belt. I even thought I'd earned my 10,000 hours badge by this point. The 10,000 hour-rule, now widely known, states that it takes about 10,000 hours of practicing a specific task to master it—and that doesn't include time spent merely gazing out the window during a conference call. Given the effort I've put in, I thought that after 10,000 hours something magical would happen. Confetti from the ceiling, perhaps?

When I still didn't feel like an expert even after so much practice, I began to investigate this 10,000-hour rule. According to Anders Ericsson, a psychologist and the originator of the theory, the hours need to be spent stretching beyond our comfort zones:

> *The development of genuine expertise requires struggle, sacrifice, and honest, often painful self-assessment. There are no shortcuts. It will take you at least a decade to achieve expertise, and you will need to invest that time wisely, by engaging in "deliberate" practice—practice that focuses on tasks beyond your current level of competence and comfort. You will need a well-informed coach not only to guide you through deliberate practice but also to help you learn how to coach yourself. Above all, if you want to achieve top performance as a manager and a leader, you've got to forget the folklore about genius that makes many people think they cannot take a scientific approach to developing expertise.*

I did a little more research and discovered that Benjamin Bloom, an education professor at the University of Chicago, had studied mastery-learning by looking at the childhoods of 120 elite performers across a wide array of disciplines. His findings?

There's no correlation between IQ and expert performance. Instead, the magic formula is this:

1. Intense practice
2. Enthusiastic support from family throughout the developing years
3. Devoted teachers to study with

I found another clue pointing me toward devoted teachers in the book, *The Craftsman* by sociologist Richard Sennett. In it, he describes the way medieval goldsmiths learned from masters. An apprentice would first earn room and board while copying what everyone else in the workshop was doing. After about seven years, if he passed a test to prove he knew how to work with the material, he became a journeyman. Wandering from workshop to workshop and learning a variety of approaches was a crucial step to becoming a master craftsman.

Reading this made me wonder if the answer to my struggle could be found by becoming a journeyman. What if I sought out new inspiration from some top performers in my field? Would anyone be game to let me shadow them? Could I somehow recruit people to invest in my development and challenge my thinking?

These questions renewed my adventurous spirit.

Although I didn't know it at the time, the seed for this idea had originally been planted nine years ago. I was working as a mid-level strategist and was due for my performance evaluation, but I had no idea whether I should be asking for a raise or not. I wanted to know not only what people with similar amounts of experience were making but also the difference between the genders, if any, because I'd read so many studies showing that women are generally paid less than men. Without an objective source of information, I had no way to ground a conversation with my boss.

So I sent out a survey to people I knew in similar positions and asked them to spread the survey among their networks too, promising them I'd publish the results. One hundred thirty people completed the survey, and I was able to negotiate a raise and a promotion for myself, based on facts rather than wishes.

I published the results and received so much positive feedback about how helpful it was that I continued to conduct the survey each year. Over time I expanded the questions to learn more about different approaches and industry perceptions, not just how much money people made. More and more people participated each year. It seemed a wealth of potential masters might be positively predisposed to let me learn from them in a journeyman-type situation.

My journeyman idea was emboldened by Stefan Sagmeister's TED talk. He spoke about the power of time off and had me mesmerized when he so eloquently described the typical linear life: twenty-five years learning, followed by forty years working, capped off with a final fifteen years of retirement. He decided to take some of those retirement years and intersperse them into his working years by taking a one-year sabbatical every seven years. During his sabbaticals, his design studio closes, and he spends an entire year conducting experiments designed to inspire the next seven years of work upon his return. As I listened to him speak, I thought, *I could do my own version of that.*

Becoming a journeyman, I reasoned, would need to be different from working, freelancing, or going back to school. The master practitioners in my field aren't ever just sitting on their hands, waiting to teach. When you're hired, it's to do a job that needs doing. Learning and developing intuition is an outcome of doing the work and having experiences rather than a boon of devoted tutelage. Freelancing rarely provides time for instructional conversations or gives you the full picture on a project. And while I might learn a lot going back to school, there is no current learning environment designed for my precise needs, somewhere between executive education and earning another master's degree. The current masters, the ones I wanted to work with, are on the front line, in jobs.

The typical method for gathering knowledge from working practitioners is to interview them for a couple of hours, resulting in an article or interview transcript in a book. I felt strongly that to uncover new approaches and new ways of working, I'd have to spend more time than an interview would allow.

I thought about the types of people I wanted to work with. Ideally, I'd have my pick from among those in the most progressive companies, or at least from the change agents swimming upstream in the more traditional companies. However, these folks would be quite busy. They wouldn't be able to drop what they were doing to work with me for eight hours a day.

So what if I set out on a more ethnographic endeavor to maximize our time together? What if I asked some innovative master practitioners to host me in their homes? I could offer them some cross-pollination, some renewed enthusiasm for their own work, and contribute to their projects. In exchange, I would see their lives more intimately by sharing commutes and weekends. These newly forged relationships might carry on beyond a couple of weeks and last throughout my career.

I sat down and e-mailed potential master craftsmen and craftswomen. I also posted the idea on my blog and mentioned it in the survey to see if there were any progressives out there I hadn't thought to approach. I explained that I'd love to spend a couple of weeks working with them and learning from them and, oh yes, staying in their house.

And the most magical thing happened.

People said yes.

And not reluctantly, either.

> *I absolutely, unconditionally, passionately love this idea.*
> *Actually "love it" doesn't do it justice; it's "leave my wife for it" adoration.*
> *(I won't tell Jill that, she might not be that happy to hear she's lost out to an idea from someone I've never met.)*
> *- Rob Campbell*

> *I have wanted to contact you for a while now.*
> *First of all: congratulations. Great move and I'm sure one day you will look back at this decision and say it was one of the best things that ever happened to your life. I want to invite you over to Beijing.*
> *- rOobin Golestan*

Yeses began rolling in from all around the globe. I was giddy. Who doesn't want to see more of the world? It's rare to find people who don't enjoy travel. They probably marry the people who don't like music. My earlier research while working on an airline account had taught me the importance of disorienting ourselves through international travel. I'd read studies that showed traveling, and especially living abroad, makes us more creative and intelligent.

I'd already experienced this secret tonic of difference and distance when I left the US and moved to the Netherlands—and even while based there, I had clients in Italy, Switzerland, and Dubai. I went to meetings in London and Berlin. I took holidays in Cyprus and Honduras. I'd already, in some sense, traveled the world and developed an appreciation for the magnificent cultural diversity on the planet.

Yet I'd never traveled to Asia. Now I could fix this.

As it turned out, nine top marketing strategists from places as different as Seattle and Shanghai agreed to this crazy proposal to let me stay with them for two weeks each. But why would anyone agree to let some unfamiliar lump of cells into their home? I was about to find out.

I had some money saved and no boyfriend to threaten to break up with me if I left Amsterdam (my home at the time). I could freelance in between my journeyman weeks and rent out my place on Airbnb to further stave off destitution. Besides, I really love taking on things that other people don't dare do. Nervous but also excited, I quit my job and started booking flights. I decided to write a book about my experiences, to help make me more disciplined about retaining all that I would learn.

I wasn't militant about rules for my experiment. This was not to be a quantitative endeavor, and with limited time on this planet I knew I wouldn't achieve a representative sample. All of my mentors ended up being Western. All but one were men. I would have liked to go to Argentina, Australia, and India as well, but I wasn't able to find hosts there.

You hold in your hands the fruit of my yearlong journey. In *Brain Surfing*, you will meet nine masters who each taught me something I might never have learned otherwise and who all broadened my approach as a strategist.

I now have a council of mentors, ranging from modern-minded to radical, who invested in me. And by writing this book, I'm investing in you. I hope you will find inspiration, new tools, and ideas within these pages that you can immediately apply to your work—and maybe even your life.

the COURAGE to begin

你好.
Néih hóu.

JASON OKE

YOUNG & RUBICAM | HONG KONG

chapter
ONE

**"Beginning well is an art form, a clearing away of
the crass and the complicated to find the beautiful, often
hidden lineaments of the essential and the necessary."**
– David Whyte

I leave Amsterdam on a day you don't leave Amsterdam. It's Queen's Day. A celebration I've participated in before where tourists and citizens swarm the streets together, a heaving orange mess of beer, boats, music, pop-up sales of used home goods, and sweat in celebration of the sitting royal's birthday. The government has placed portable toilets around the city, but there's always someone peeing in a doorway, someone else vomiting. I'm happy to flee.

My journeyman's adventure begins in Hong Kong, and when I land, I find I'm suddenly the tallest person in sight. Holland is one of the few places I've been in the world where people don't stare or make frequent comments about my being six feet tall, but there are no eyes on me here either. Holding onto the overhead bar of the airport shuttle, I look at my reflection in the glass: dirty-blonde, fair-skinned, with green eyes—clearly not Asian. I thought more people would be staring at me, the flamingo that I am.

I'm surprised I'm not nervous—this isn't just another business trip. I'm here to work with Jason Oke, newly minted managing director for Y&R—Young & Rubicam Hong Kong. I switch on my phone and let him know I've landed safely as I proceed to follow the instructions he sent earlier over e-mail: They direct me to take one short train ride and then a taxi ride. At the train station, I discover English is the default language on the ticket machine. Hong Kong is almost too easy to maneuver.

After switching from the train to a cab, I tell the driver the name of Jason's apartment building, and I'm whipped around the huge mountains. The car is surrounded by tropical green. As we wind around the island, dodging cyclists, I can see the sea and feel the warm air.

GUINEA PIG NUMBER ONE

It was fitting to start my project in Hong Kong because Asian cultures have a heritage of respecting masters. The Western world has adopted and romanticized many Eastern terms for "teacher": Think guru, sensei, or Zen master.

But it was also fitting because, although I didn't yet know it, what Jason was about to teach me were the skills for how to dive into new projects.

Coming up in my working life, I'd always thought the goal was to reach the point where getting started on a new project would be a snap. I wouldn't hesitate, and I'd feel completely confident about the right research to do and the right questions to ask. By this point in my life, I certainly knew things to do, but with strategy, as in life, there is never just one right answer. Every new beginning requires courage.

Jason is the ideal first coach to work with. His experience spans a number of agencies with a variety of clients. Having left his Canadian origins to come to Asia, he's now in the midst of making another transition from strategy director to managing director. Given the constant challenges he's tackled in his career, I am most eager to learn how he has overcome any insecurity so that I might develop skills to tackle my own.

The taxi arrives at a high-rise apartment building set on a cliff above the waves. I wheel my suitcase into the lobby where I'm greeted by Jason and the two most adorable smiles, belonging to Millie, five, and Dash, three.

"Hello!" says Jason, taking my suitcase. "How was the trip?"

Millie and Dash hide behind Jason's legs.

"Everything went smoothly. I can't believe I'm here," I say. "Your view must be incredible."

"Come on in and see for yourself."

Jason leads us to the elevator and we ascend to the twenty-eighth floor. It's Sunday evening, and I've arrived just before the kids' bedtime.

"Hi, Heather!" Meredith, Jason's wife, says as we enter the apartment.

The Okes' three-bedroom apartment opens onto the dining area and the living room. There's a wall of windows looking down on the rocks and swirling sea. Jason gives me a quick tour. The modern furnishings and children's toys here and there are completely upstaged by the view. The family shows me to the guest room where I'll be staying. It looks out on the same epic view.

"Millie, Dash, I brought you something," I say, unzipping my suitcase.

They come closer, and I pull out two pairs of wooden shoes.

"Those are funny shoes!" Millie says as I place them on the floor in front of her and Dash.

"That's what shoes look like where Heather comes from," Meredith tells them. "Why don't you try them on and Daddy can take your picture?"

The kids clomp around on the wood floors in the strange shoes, giggling. I hope, in my desire to woo the kids, I haven't brought the equivalent of a drum set into the Okes' home.

Meredith wrangles the kids into their room for a story before bed, and Jason and I go into the kitchen where he orders some takeout. The housekeeper's room is just off the back of the kitchen, but today is her day off. She'll be back in the morning.

I'm exhausted from the flight and the time difference, so after a quick dinner of stir-fry and rice they kindly let me sneak off to the guest room. We'll leave for the office at seven thirty the next morning.

I wake to the sounds of Dash and Millie padding around the apartment, laughing and talking. Monday morning means school for Millie.

Out in the hallway, I find Virginia, the fifty-something Indonesian live-in housekeeper, in the hallway, gently persuading Dash to put on clothes. I greet her and the kids and slip into the bathroom, which has a shower curtain sporting an aquarium scene. It feels strange to be in someone else's space, but going through the morning routine helps to push those feelings aside.

I quickly pull myself together, and when I come out, I see Jason has a "dad goes to work" look: pressed, colorful, plaid button-down shirt with cuff links. He picks up Dash and holds him upside down while the little boy giggles and squirms. Once we sit down to eat some muesli and yogurt, Millie teaches us how to count in Cantonese—*yuht, yee, sahm.*

"You are the most smartest, Millie-girl," Jason praises.

Then Meredith gathers Millie's things and pushes us all out the door and down the elevator. We put Millie on her shuttle bus and board our own bus behind it.

We're both trying not to feel awkward, but we've only spent a total of about thirty minutes together in person before this, and that was two years ago. At the time, we were online acquaintances, and thanks to Foursquare, we realized we were both on Madison Avenue at the same time, so we met for a quick chat and a glass of water on a steamy July day. Today is a similarly humid day in Hong Kong, and I'm just a tall, blonde, single girl he met on the Internet who's following him to work.

The minibus sweeps us back out onto the road, curving through lush greenery until we're crossing a bridge over a massive reservoir. It's a breathtaking view of rolling green hills and calm water.

"Not bad, is it?" Jason says.

He's from Toronto, but so far I haven't heard a single "eh?"

Nature quickly transforms to city, and we're deposited at the bottom of a hill and are carried with a swarm of people into the metro station. The metro ride lasts only a few minutes, and we get off at Quarry Bay.

In this part of town, the buildings tower over us, high above the ground floors' storefronts. Familiar outposts such as Pizza Hut, McDonald's, and Starbucks appear as we walk, interspersed with dry cleaners and very small, somewhat dingy cafés. One of the buildings is entirely covered with a web of bamboo scaffolding, indicating it's under construction.

We round the corner and enter a large glass office building. There's a queue for the elevator.

Four attendants donning white gloves direct traffic into the four different elevators. They assist in quality control to make sure no elevator is too full.

"We're fancy," Jason says as we wait our turn. "No pushing elevator buttons for you."

We ride to the thirty-second floor in a mirrored enclosure. I feel like I should be wearing a business suit with very large shoulder pads in a bold primary color.

The Y&R office is a sea of empty desks. Jason prefers to arrive early and get a jump-start on the day, but he's one of the few, he tells me. Most employees still live at home with their extended family, so they choose to start a bit later and then stay in the office in the evenings where they have the luxury of air-conditioning, high-speed Internet, and no grandmother asking when they're going to get married.

Jason's office is on the perimeter with one wall made of floor-to-ceiling windows like at his home. I go straight toward it and look down at Victoria Harbor, peppered with barges and ferries. Across the water are more skyscrapers and mountains.

"You must get sick of all these views," I say.

Jason pulls his laptop from his bag to place it in the one empty space among the stacks of folders and rows of books on his desk. He has a picture of Meredith and the kids on his desk. There are drawings the kids have done pinned to a board next to work papers.

"Let's have you sit here." He directs me to a desk just outside his office where we can still see each other.

As I'm setting up my own laptop, the office tea/coffee lady, Kei Tse, delivers Jason's usual and then turns to me, expectant but silent.

"Choose wisely," Jason tells me. "She has a mind like a trap."

Since it's Monday morning, the first thing to do is attend the weekly status meeting. Jason has been in Hong Kong, and at Y&R, for just over two years as the Regional Head of Strategy for Asia, but more recently he has assumed the role of managing director. This is just one of the reasons I'm so keen to work with him. There are quite a few skilled strategists who have made the transition to this type of role. Is this a path I might pursue too? Through this project, I'm hoping to explore all of the ladders I might climb. There's certainly some appeal to the idea of being captain.

After checking a few e-mails and seeing Jason's colleagues filter in, Jason leads me to the main conference room. It's very classic and could be anywhere in the world, if not for the view of the bay and mountains, framed on two sides by the distinctive buildings.

As the big cheese, Jason takes a chair at the head of the table while the rest of the team fills the other seats, chatting about their weekends.

I introduce myself to Caroline, head of client services, and she reveals, in a warm but reserved English accent, that she's just returned from a weekend trip to Thailand. On my other side is Valentina, the head of shopper marketing, who is quite the Italian character and has the fashion to match: She's wearing a killer blue dress and impossibly high heels. Shen, the creative director, swoops into the room. His style is more relaxed: just a T-shirt and jeans.

He takes his post next to Jason, who begins the meeting by introducing me, saying that I'll be following him around for a couple of weeks for a book I'm writing. He seems a little self-conscious, and his news raises a few eyebrows. Their boss must be pretty special if someone is writing a book about him.

They dive into a massive spreadsheet, projected to the front of the room, and begin talking through a number of projects for Colgate, their largest client. Jason digs into the launch work they are doing for a fruit-flavored toothpaste.

"What's happening on Fruity?" he asks.

There are several bright sparks who update the room on the ins and outs of the clients' requests and the possible solutions. The meeting is conducted in perfect English. When Hong Kong was handed over to China, ending British rule in the late '90s, many Hong Kong families moved to the US and Canada. The children of those families were educated there, but many have now returned to Hong Kong. The result is a workforce that speaks both English and Cantonese fluently.

Jason questions a line item on the spreadsheet. "Can someone ask our robot overlords where these objectives came from?"

He then sets off an impassioned critique of some of the recent briefs and the tendency to write vague rather than measurable objectives. One project catches his attention, and he highlights it for us. "Well," he says, "it may not make sense, but this is good. Somebody somewhere is doing some math."

Setting measurable objectives is the one thing almost everyone can agree is crucial in starting a project. But how else do you get going?

CHECKLISTS AND COACHES

Snooping through Jason's bookshelf in his office while we chat that first afternoon, I discover that we both own Atul Gawande's *The Checklist Manifesto*. In it, Gawande describes the increasing complexity of the medical profession resulting in a proliferation of specialties. Despite the rise in doctors' specialized knowledge, Gawande was surprised to learn that there hadn't been a corresponding decline in surgical mistakes. Errors were still happening all too often in his estimation, and other experts agreed with him. So Gawande stole the concept of the humble checklist from the world of aviation and applied it to medicine. In a yearlong pilot study, eight hospitals worldwide implemented his idea of using a simple two-minute, nineteen-point checklist prior to surgery: As a result, deaths went down by 47 percent, complications went down by 36%, and infection decreased by almost half.

I pull the book off the shelf. "I love and hate the idea of applying this idea to strategy work," I say. "On the one hand, it would have made the first five years of working so much less ambiguous. But then, there just aren't certain things that you should *always* do on any given project."

"That book really inspired me," Jason tells me. "I put together this list of fifty ways to get started, just for those first moments when there's so much you could do that it's almost paralyzing. In those moments, it's best to do anything to help you learn about the brand and what people are currently doing in the category. So it's more like a serendipity list than a checklist. You could pick any number and try that item just to see where it leads you."

How simple is that? His list (*see Fifty Ways to Get Started*) covers both digital and analog sources of inspiration, and he even appropriates the religious slogan with "What would Jon Steel do?"

Ulli Appelbaum, founder of the consultancy First the Trousers Then the Shoes Inc., was similarly inspired to create a tool he calls Positioning Roulette by analyzing over 1,200 case studies from around the world. He identified twenty-six possible approaches brands can take, such as identifying an enemy or submitting the brand to a torture test. He also built a handy website (positioning-roulette.com) outlining approaches that are full of provocative questions to stimulate thinking.

A former colleague at The Martin Agency, Fritz Kuhn, used to talk young strategists off the ledge by saying, "Remember, we're not putting hearts in babies." So I get that these lists are not likely to save any lives, but they can help anyone get a more elegant and less panicky start on things.

Talking about Gawande reminded me of one of my favorite articles, "Coaching a Surgeon," which Gawande wrote for *The New Yorker*. I mention it to Jason, and it turns out he connects deeply with it too. In the article, Gawande makes the observation that professional athletes have coaches, but the rest of us? We're somehow meant to muddle through on our own.

Recognizing this, Gawande (at that time, eight years in as a practicing surgeon) went back to his residency mentor and asked him to come and observe Gawande's surgeries and critique them. His mentor would stand on a stool, watch Gawande's work, and then afterward share his insights, such as how the way that Gawande draped the patient limited his access to the surgical site, or how it had taken too long for Gawande to notice that the operating light wasn't centered on the incision.

I hoped to gain this kind of insight into my own ways of working by doing this brain-surfing project, but Jason saw the beauty of my project being the reverse.

"It's like you're the observer, and we are Atul Gawande in the operating room," he says. "All of a sudden, we're noticing our own bad habits and corner cutting and lazy thinking in a new light because there's someone watching. For me that's a good thing. If slightly terrifying."

By "standing on the stool" and not being the boss, I would have the opportunity to interrogate someone else's approach—someone very senior and with lots of different experience to mine. I realized that for the past few years, I'd worked mostly with my adjacent peers in other disciplines or with younger strategists who reported to me. There's a different power dynamic between Jason and me, because there's no professional hierarchy and because the host/guest dynamic fosters a spirit of openness.

"I have a coach back in Toronto," Jason says. "He spent thirty years working in advertising and knows a thing or two about our business. No matter where I am in the world, I try to keep our weekly call."

"So I'm not the first person to stand on the stool for you?" I say, mock-hurt.

If people as successful as Jason and Gawande use coaches, that says to me that we can all benefit from finding an expert who will critique us. Up to this point, I've always relied on my supervisors to give me this sort of feedback, but now I realize I hunger for more than an annual performance evaluation or the occasional course-correct and "'atta-girl.'"

"We're dealing with ambiguity where there is no one right answer," Jason tells me. "So talking to a coach gives me perspective."

INANE QUESTIONS AND LIMP EXERCISES

I quickly adapt to Jason's schedule: On weeknights, he makes it home just as the kids are going to bed or after they're already asleep. We eat the dinner Virginia has prepared and drink wine while we chat.

On Tuesday, we sip some cabernet, sitting in the living room, and I ask, "What surprising things have happened in your career?"

"Well, remember how blogging really blew up around 2004, 2005? I made one comment on Malcolm Gladwell's blog that several people picked up on. It's funny how one little comment could raise your profile back then."

Gladwell had reviewed Charles Tilly's book *Why?*, which describes the different ways people respond to questions and how we're all prone to respond with conventions or post-rationalizations when we cannot express our emotions. In his comment, Jason related his frustration with focus groups, an oft-used tool to research customer opinions. Lots of people responded and reblogged this comment. It also got Jason invited to give talks and even contribute a chapter to a marketing textbook. Here's the magical quote:

> *I think, as I gather you do, that how we feel about a brand, and which products and services we choose, is usually explained by a fantastically complex set of factors: the brands our parents used, the brands we see people around us use, the image of the brand, our personal experience with it, a sale, a half-remembered ad from 10 years ago, and so on. This is probably best explained as a story—we may both buy Tide, but there's a different narrative that brought each of us to pick it up.*

> *But in market research, the answers people give sound more like conventions: "It's a good value," "my family likes it," "it tastes good." And it seems that because of the artificiality of the situation, the perils of introspection, etc., most market research actually encourages people to answer in conventions, and doesn't encourage the telling of stories. Many of these stories are probably complex and deeply buried such that they are hard to consciously access anyway.*

Market research can be traced back to the 1920s, when it began with direct, literal question-and-answer surveying of customers and potential customers. It remained popular for many years, but over time it has become clearer that these types of survey questions have their limits. While there's no indication that focus groups as a methodology are waning just yet, they are generally reviled among my strategist peers for the reasons Jason raised in his comment.

He fills my glass with his right hand and gesticulates with his left, growing impassioned: "We know—I mean we really *know*—that focus group findings are not very useful. Focus groups are akin to strip-mining people's heads. People are bored by the idea of sitting in a dimly lit room for two hours being poked at with inane questions and limp exercises."

One piece of evidence against the typical focus group stems from the ground-breaking work of Dr. Robert Heath, originator of the theory of low-involvement processing. He theorized that not only do we rarely engage our conscious mind to process most communication about brands, we in fact rely on ingrained memory structures to make our brand decisions. The idea that people rationally debate each feature of competing brands is an illusion. And yet in most focus groups, that's the underlying assumption because the research only interrogates the rational portion of the brain.

"So how do you get the kind of information you need to inspire new strategies?" I ask.

"Plan research that doesn't make people invent reasons around their unconscious motivations. Ask people to be creative instead. There are also projective techniques, like the classic tombstone exercise, as in, What would it say on the brand's tombstone? But I've also asked people to pretend they're the company's marketing department and they have to come up with advertising ideas. It's more useful for me to see people be creative so I can draw from their unique personal experience. That's where inspiration comes from, stuff that you've never heard before, instead of the predictable mind-numbing things people think they're supposed to say about a particular product or brand. And the thing is, once clients get a taste for good research, they won't want the other kind."

I already knew about these particular techniques as I've used them with some clients. Jason and I have both had success creating custom panels of customers who we interacted with over longer periods of time. New technologies like MindSwarms—where participants take short video clips of themselves answering questions while at home or in a store—go a step further, providing a window into people's lives. These tools bring in quick input and let us feel what customers feel by seeing the world through their eyes.

As I turn in for the night, I reflect on all the hours of research I've conducted over the years. What I haven't done is stick up for good research when clients insist on bad. I've never truly fought with a client, never been kicked off an account, and never been fired. When clients have rejected my proposed method for intelligence gathering, these are the things I feared. That was me being collaborative, right? Or do I acquiesce too soon? I have certainly been in the unenviable scenario after conducting research where we haven't learned much that we didn't already know.

This introspection with Jason has made me realize that good research is a critical element to beginning a project well and is worth fighting for.

A TALE OF TWO ROBOTS

At the end of our first week, Jason offers to show me a talk he put together especially for clients with zero risk tolerance. We come back to his office after a nice dim sum lunch. Gazing out the window, I see ferries and barges go about their business in the bay below.

Jason turns his laptop so I can see from across his desk.

"I met this NASA rocket scientist on a plane, Dave Lavery. He really does wear Hawaiian shirts." Jason points to a picture of a man in a Hawaiian shirt on the screen.

On the flight, Jason and Dave got to discussing the development of the rover NASA sent to collect samples on Mars. NASA started out by designing a robot that was as big as a truck and chock-full of computers. The robot, which they called Robby, would take a bunch of pictures, render them into a 3-D image, and then decide if it should collect a sample or move forward twelve inches before initiating the sequence again. It was heinously slow and cost $2 billion to build.

NASA was stumped. Should they send this expensive and slow robot to Mars? How much will it be able to see of Mars before breaking down?

Enter Collin, the intern. Collin was overeager and always asking to help out, so Dave explained the problem to him, and Collin went home over the weekend, spent five hundred bucks at RadioShack, and built a prototype robot the size of a large radio-control called Tooth.

He had to beg the NASA guys to put Tooth through the tests they were using for the rover, but when they finally did, Tooth blew all the tests away. It had no computers and just tried to grab anything it could, or it would reverse and change course if it couldn't go forward. And Tooth was the model that was eventually perfected and sent to Mars.

"I think most companies operate like Robby," Jason tells me. "They want to achieve 100 percent perfect knowledge before making a decision. But I think we'd be better off behaving more like Tooth. We should get out there and be responsive based on what we come across. We need to be more reactive to our environment.

"A lot of companies have a hard time behaving like Tooth because they're locked into a twelve-month marketing calendar, or they've committed to doing a promotion with a retailer six months in advance. But I have to question the wisdom of rigid plans made far in advance, because we'll never have perfect foresight no matter how much research we do."

This brings to mind some of my favorite examples of companies being agile and nimble when it comes to marketing. One is Duracell, which brought in branded mobile charging stations to New York City for citizens trapped without power after Hurricane Sandy. Another is Unilever in India, which was quick to make the best of a controversial situation after former cricketer Michael Vaughan accused batsman VVS Laxman of doctoring his bat with Vaseline for an unfair advantage. Unilever responded by blanketing key publications in India with a print ad that defended Laxman and touted the beneficial uses of its product on skin rather than on cricket bats. Saving some budget for these unexpected opportunities allows brands to step up when the right moment arises.

Cultural anthropologist Grant McCracken calls actions such as these and other timely experiments Culturematics. He wrote a book by the same name on the subject, where he recommends putting out low-cost, playful ideas into the world. If we don't, he warns, we'll be left behind, because it's almost impossible to know what the next compelling and spreadable idea will be.

When I worked with Burger King, we executed many small ideas alongside the big, expensive traditional advertising elements. We called this "lighting lots of fires." For example, we launched several ideas all at the same time: Whopper Sacrifice, Whopper Virgins, and Whopper Flame. These were cohesive ideas, rather than one "matching luggage" idea retold in every media channel. This bravery on the clients' part made it possible for Whopper Sacrifice to earn upward of $150,000 in unpaid media. The app, which cost $10,000 to build, asked you to prove you love the Whopper more than those superfluous Facebook friends we all have by giving you a free Whopper after you unfriended ten people. It tapped into a current cultural phenomenon and at the same time rubbed against the ethos of Facebook—so much so that Facebook took it down after two weeks, yielding even more press.

But Whopper Flame? You've rightly never heard of it. How were we to know, *for certain*, that a designer fragrance inspired by the Whopper and sold in a pop-up retail store in Times Square would bomb? Maybe if it actually smelled of burgers it would have done better.

Campaigns such as these are more Tooth than Robby. And I think that's a lovely way to think about it, because there's power in both approaches.

WOO THE DISLOYAL

Jonny Lang, not the blues singer but the head of strategy from the Y&R Singapore office, is also in Hong Kong at the moment, pitching in on some Colgate projects. Jonny has a lot of technology experience and loves helping brands to see their potential beyond above-the-line channels such as TV and print.

Jason asks us to have a look at a campaign that the Colgate client loves that is entirely above-the-line. Is there a way to extend it into digital channels? Can we encourage people to "engage" with their toothpaste?

Jason acknowledges that this is a backward request. Ideally, we wouldn't be trying to translate an idea across channels. Instead, the channels or technology aspects should emerge naturally from the start. Jonny and I embrace the assignment regardless, and we riff easily off each other's ideas.

In Asia, where mass media is still quite cheap and effective, digital campaigns are more nascent. There are trade-offs between different courses of action. Which is better? $300K spent on a microsite that 40K people visit, or that same money spent on TV flights that can reach twenty million people?

After just a couple of hours' work, Jonny and I have some ideas we're pretty excited to share with Jason. We walk over to Jason's office and take him through our thoughts. Like us, Jason is most excited about our idea to create a dating site where profile pictures of smiles are the only ones allowed. We munch on some beef jerky that Jonny brought from Singapore, and the conversation turns toward how digital ideas are treated in Asia.

"In the echo chamber of adland, we treat engagement as an unalloyed good," Jason says. "No matter how you look at any of the data that's ever been gathered, behavior on the Internet has a long-tail distribution. There are a lot of people doing very little—lurking, liking—and very few people contributing a lot—blogging, uploading videos."

It's true. No argument from me. Jonny is nodding along, too.

"You see the long-tail is mirrored in purchases compared to 'likes,'" Jonny adds. "For any brand, way more people buy the product than 'like' the brand on Facebook."

"Heather," Jason says, "have you read *How Brands Grow* by Byron Sharp?"

I shake my head and jot down the title in my notebook. Jason explains that Sharp is the lead disciple of the Ehrenberg-Bass Institute, a marketing think tank in Australia. He pulls the book from his shelf, searches for a specific page, and then sets it between Jonny and me across the desk so we can see a chart that dispels the 80:20 rule. Rather than 20 percent of customers accounting for 80 percent of sales, the vast majority of sales come from people who buy the brand once or maybe twice a year. The number of people who buy only one brand every time they shop, Sharp concludes, is very, very low.

"People just don't care that much about brands," Jason says. He opens a presentation to reference Colgate data from China as an example. "Ninety-nine percent in this sample have bought Colgate at least once." I wonder who makes up that last one percent of holdouts, but Jason moves on.

"The number of people aware of the brand drops off a bit from there, and the number aware of the advertising is a bit lower still. The numbers keep sliding down as you look at top-of-mind awareness and then at the percent of people who can give any information about the brand (key color, any advertising, the benefits). Only a third of people can come up with any of these specific details about the brand."

This amazes me, given that virtually *everybody* has actually used the brand. Market share in China for Colgate is about 15 percent, but the number of people who insist "this is the only brand I use" is less than 1 percent.

"The number of people who have real knowledge about Colgate, let alone passion for it, is very low," Jonny says.

"What Sharp has impressed on me," Jason adds, "is that not many people actually know or care that much about brands—even the people that use them regularly."

Andrew Ehrenberg, the think tank co-namesake, discovered a pattern that's true for almost every brand in every category in almost every country in the world: It demonstrates the large proportion of people who just don't care. It's called negative binomial distribution, and it means that most of the purchases are made by light buyers (one or two or three purchases per year), and then the long-tail emerges with fewer and fewer heavy buyers making four, five, six, or more purchases of a brand per year. This is how markets are structured, and this is how people buy in large categories where there's competition. Colgate and Crest exhibit the exact same pattern; it's just that the number of light buyers starts a bit higher for Crest, and thus they're the market leader.

The negative binomial distribution maps back to the digital conversation when you overlay the long-tail buyer-distribution chart with the long-tail knowledge-of-the-brand chart and the long-tail number-of-people-participating-with-a-brand chart. The group of people who contribute the most revenue to a brand don't actually know that much about the brand, because they only buy once, maybe twice a year, nor are they likely to "engage" with the content a brand is creating.

Ehrenberg-Bass studies have looked at Facebook fans and found that fans are generally comprised of the people who are already loyal and passionate about a brand.

"You talk to a Facebook rep," Jonny says, "and they say, 'We've done research that shows that Facebook fans are way more loyal and buy your brand way more often.' The conclusion they're pushing us toward is that we need to get more fans, because fans are loyal and buy."

"I get it," I chime in. "It's been burned into my brain as much as yours: Correlation does not equal causation. Facebook is just twisting the argument for their own benefit."

"Right," Jason says, "because in reality, the best way to get more Facebook fans is to get more people buying your brand. Surprisingly though, if you want to grow your brand, you don't grow it by focusing on loyalty. Crest in China is about 50 percent bigger than Colgate. The vast majority of the difference is among the people who buy one to three times per year. Crest is a much bigger brand so people buy it more often. If Colgate wants to grow, we just need to get people to buy it once or twice per year instead of none or once."

Essentially, there are never two brands with the same market share but drastically different loyalty rates. You'll never find an instance where one brand has half the market penetration of another brand but twice the loyalty, and thus the same market share. If you do, Byron Sharp wants you to contact him.

Sharp isn't the only one asserting that market-share growth depends on growing the customer base, not on increasing loyalty. In the book *Marketing in the Era of Accountability*, Les Binet and Peter Field analyzed 880 campaign case studies from the database of all cases submitted to the IPA Effectiveness Awards. The analysis revealed that the case studies that won—the ones that convinced a panel of judges beyond a reasonable doubt that the campaigns in question achieved a good financial return—set out to increase penetration. Even the cases that claimed the objective was to increase loyalty actually ended up increasing penetration.

"Man, this is really eye-opening for me," I say. "When I worked on Burger King, our strategy documents identified the Super Fan as the target—people in the US who eat fast food nine or more times per month. We thought our goal was to encourage people who ate at Burger King once or twice out of those nine times to go two or three times instead. We were aiming to improve loyalty.

"I believe our work was effective in driving sales because Burger King had twenty consecutive quarters of increased sales while partnered with Crispin Porter + Bogusky. But according to Sharp, we should have been working toward penetration instead of loyalty. We should have been striving to get people to eat out more and making it easier for people to think of Burger King when they did."

As I reflect on this conversation and think about the campaigns I was a part of at CP+B, I can see how we actually *were* increasing penetration and not just loyalty. The silly masculine themes didn't just appeal to the predominantly male Super Fans; women also found them funny. The broad mass-media spend behind the TV spots full of food porn reached all kinds of people, not just Super Fans. We pressed various need states and highlighted new eating occasions with lighter items, late-night availability, breakfast, and snacks. And the new products developed over these years were novel, high-fat, high-sugar items. They targeted anyone with a lizard brain.

Was there any evidence of increased loyalty? As I think about it, it dawns on me that there's just not that much more fast food that Super Fans could possibly consume, and the convenience of more McDonald's and Subway locations, plus the Super Fan's natural drive to seek out variety, makes them naturally disloyal.

Thinking about this Burger King work in a new light is an awakening for me. Now I see that my objectives going forward for any brand should be to grow the customer base and to make the brand easier to buy for more people in more situations. These are the big drivers of market share.

Later, when I have a chance to read *How Brands Grow*, I see that Sharp describes modern-day marketers as medieval doctors proffering bloodletting with no evidence of its efficacy. That's because his research has led to eleven "empirical generalizations," otherwise known as laws, that he explains and shares the data behind their discovery.

While I get the importance of learning about such patterns, I think it's important to note that they're not all-inclusive guidelines for every marketing challenge we'll ever face. Almost all of his evidence has been collected from packaged-goods brands. These laws reflect data from established brands rather than explain brands like Red Bull that come out of nowhere and catch the cultural wave. He criticizes loyalty schemes as discounts for people who would likely buy a product anyway, but he doesn't acknowledge the new reality of apps such as Starbucks' with billions of dollars of cash flow provided by customers who store money to spend in the future. And how can we create the quick rise in participation witnessed in social-good events like Movember or the Ice Bucket Challenge? How do we explain those rare brands like Rolls-Royce that don't really market themselves, with products we may hardly ever see in person (unless you live in Miami or Dubai), and yet have a huge share of the public's awareness? There are still a lot of laws left to uncover.

MORPHING INTO A MANAGING DIRECTOR

Jason and I head home in a taxi to save some time on the commute. The late afternoon is steamy, and the vinyl of the seat sticks to the back of my legs. It's the end of my trip, and the last I'll see of these modern winding roads that hug wild, lush greenery. I fly in the morning, and because Jason and Meredith have a fancy dinner-and-dancing fund-raiser for Millie's school tonight, I've made plans to meet a friend and see some Hong Kong nightlife.

Jason rolls up his sleeves in an attempt to cool off and asks, "Any lingering questions? You ready to move to Hong Kong?"

"I think you've got an enviable life here, that's for sure," I say. "I guess I'm left wondering if the MD role is something to strive for?"

"Well, for me, the managing director job has been an entrée into this whole new confusing world in the same way Asia was when we moved here. That was a humbling experience," he says. "There were so many things to learn, so much novelty to experience. That fun and excitement has happened again in this new role. I'm stepping into the unknown lands of managing a budget and loads of people.

"It's so easy to get stuck in the ruts and habits of life. Being a novice again reminds me that life is not about getting comfortable. I see your project in the same vein. It's hard to get comfortable when you decide to fling yourself into other workplaces and countries."

Peeling my legs off the seat to get more comfortable, I ask Jason, "Did you seek any advice when the MD role came up?"

"I talked to Rob White of Zeus Jones, and he told me, 'Don't stop being a strategist. Don't think you have to all of a sudden forget everything you've ever learned just because your job title changed. Take the strategic skills and figure out how to apply them to these new situations.'

"I realized that these skills I'd developed are valuable, especially in business and managing an agency. Like, how to be curious, to listen, to find patterns and separate signal from noise. How to connect disparate ideas, to find creative solutions, to get a thought or argument down to its essence. And, most important, how to post-rationalize like a motherfucker."

Rob White's advice also made the prospect of moving into the new role less intimidating for Jason. He could look for patterns in the financial statements in the same way he used to dig through a brand tracking study. He would get to apply his understanding of psychology and mass behavior to a group of employees rather than a communications brief. Those parallel experiences give him more confidence as he sees just how transferable his skills are.

"I think lots of strategists I know would make good leaders," Jason says, smiling. "Hint, hint; nudge, nudge."

I'm humbled that Jason would imply that about me. "What's been the biggest surprise for you in this new job?"

"The mountains of minutiae: signing expenses, approving payroll, reviewing contracts, preparing agency fee actualizations, dealing with timesheets and vacation requests. That sort of shit is important but less fun, for sure. I think it's probably like being a pilot: a lot of boring routine work that you still have to pay attention to, and be present and mindful when you're doing it, because a small mistake can mean a lot of money or a lot of people's time."

I see now that there is an element of serendipity that brought Jason to where he is today. When this promotion came, rather than crafting a sadistic plot to rule over others, he was ready to say "thank you." Jason simply did his job well and collaborated with those around him. The good things fell into place from there.

Next thing I know, we're back at the Okes' "Wavy Piano Building" (that's how their apartment building is referred to in Cantonese), racing to get ready for the evening. I take a picture of Meredith and Jason decked out in their gala-wear. Smelling Meredith's perfume and seeing the kids in pajamas happily reminds me of when my own parents would prepare to go out for the night, kissing us on the head and turning on their heels toward temporary freedom.

Later, my night of bars, dinner, and late-night congee (a savory porridge popular here) has me creeping back into the Okes' house after 2:00 a.m., knowing I need to leave for the airport in less than five hours. Canadians really do leave their doors unlocked.

The entire time I've been with the Okes, the kids have woken up before 6:00 a.m., but the next morning when I get up, they're sleeping in for once. Knowing how precious sleep is in this house, I leave a goodbye note and slip out the front door.

Jason sends me an e-mail a few days later saying that Dash had wandered around the apartment that day asking, "Where's heaven? Where's heaven?" Jason

and Meredith had thought he was getting all existential and that they needed to
have a serious talk about death and dying, until they realized he'd been trying
to say my name.

FIFTY WAYS
to
get started

BY JASON OKE

1. Use the formula:

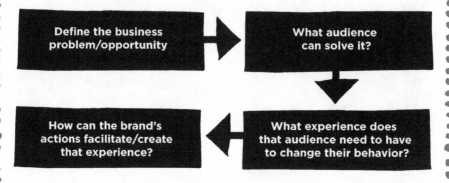

Define the business problem/opportunity	→	What audience can solve it?
How can the brand's actions facilitate/create that experience?	←	What experience does that audience need to have to change their behavior?

2. Google Trends, Google Insights, Google Suggest.

3. What archetypes does/could the brand play?

4. Review universal human needs—where does the brand make a difference to people?

5. Search planning blogs on the Plannersphere search engine.

6. Search WARC.

7. John Griffiths' Planning Kata:
   www.planningaboveandbeyond.com/planningcraft/kata

8. Search Youtube/Addictomatic/Flickr/Twitter/Delicious for the topic/brand.

9. What brand in the category has the most Facebook likes? The most Twitter followers? The fewest? Why?

10. Go to a store. Check out the retail environment. Use the actual product and the competition's.

11. Watch people buy/shop. Why does it happen the way it happens? They could have taken more time to get their bearings, or less time. They might have gone down a different aisle. They might have picked up more items, or not as many. They might have sought help from an employee. They might have, but they didn't. Look for how people enter the activity you're trying to observe, and how they exit. What's going on just before and just afterward? How do they get to the point you're interested in? What and who do they bring with them? What mental state are they in? How do they leave? What do they take with them and what do they leave behind?

12. Go somewhere else and watch the audience live their lives (the subway, the bus, the movie theatre, a restaurant, a bar, a coffee shop, a dance club).

13. Why do people use the category? Triggers: What got them to join/ start? Motivation: What keeps them going? Reinforcement: What sustains the cycle?

14. Disruption: What are the category conventions? What are the sacred cows? What MUST brands do, what MUSTN'T brands do?

15. Own the data: How often do people buy the category?
How often do they shop? How many brands do they consider?
How long does it take them to choose? How many brands do they
purchase regularly? How long is the purchase cycle? How price
sensitive are they? What are the patterns?

16. David Hackworthy's brand exercises—extreme positionings, etc.

17. Does the brand have a purpose? Do the Dove exercise:
"We believe the world would be a better place if . . . "

18. What is the brand's secret? What is the brand's gift to its users?
What tension does the brand address in culture/society?

19. How would another brand solve this problem? What
would Nike/Virgin/Starbucks/Apple/Walmart/Target do?

20. Peer brand exercise: What brands would this brand be friends with?
Who would we hang out with? Who would we totally diss?

21. Who is the REAL target? People who buy the product for someone
else? People who request the product but don't buy it themselves? It
could also be Who talks about the product? Who hates the product?
Who sells the product (e.g. internal sales force, Walmart category
buyers, etc.)?

22. Does the brand/product enhance or signal social position/
status to others? The Big Five personality dimensions: openness,
conscientiousness, agreeableness, stability, and extroversion.

23. Where are the high-status/low-status points in the category?

24. Watch some videos of other people talking about the subject.

25. Read a marketing article you've saved in Instapaper.

26. Search your old hard drive/Dropbox documents—
you've probably dealt with this problem before.

27. What about this brand is most INTERESTING?

28. What do people feel passionate about in the category?
What do they love? What do they hate? What do they fear?
What do they crave? What do they share? What do they
complain about? What do they brag about?

29. Embrace your weakest point—What's the worst/most vulnerable/
weakest part of the brand? Can we turn that on its head? Can we
fix it? Can we tell a story about fixing it? Can we challenge the
perception behind it?

30. What's happening in culture that's current/relevant/interesting
and could be associated with our brand/category?

31. Different sources for product stories/proof/RTBs: history (founder
stories, length of existence); demonstrated superiority (3x more
effective); logic chain persuasion (e.g. 3 clear reasons to choose us);
popularity (#1 brand); testimonials (why others chose us); authority
(choice of experts); guarantees (we stand behind our product).

32. Whose endorsement/recommendation matters most to this
audience? People like me (familiarity)? People I like (friendship)?
People I want to be like (aspiration)?

33. Draw out John Grant's molecules for the brand.

34. What's the brand story/narrative? What's the target
audience narrative? How do the two fit together?

35. Do something cool—give a bunch of artists and conceptual designers and teenagers and mad scientists and hackers your product and ask them what they'd do with it.

36. Grant McCracken's Culturematic formula: "What if we _____?" Do something crazy then document it and publicize it, e.g. Gatorade Replay.

37. What communities exist around the category/brand? What communities exist within the target audience? "Ask not what communities can do for your brand; ask what your brand can do for communities." People need stuff to be social around. Create social objects.

38. Be interesting, be useful, be nice, be unexpected, be helpful.

39. Switch media. Stop using the computer, write it out by hand. Dash it off quickly in bullet point form—15-minute time limit. Draw shit out. With a Sharpie and a pad. Draw a picture. Use a whiteboard. Be multimodal. Stay away from PowerPoint. Unless you absolutely have to.

40. Try writing an idea out in different lengths: a word, a sentence, a paragraph, and a page.

41. What would Jon Steel do?

42. Go for a walk, or sit still and meditate, and calm your mind.

43. Go exercise.

44. Go sleep on it.

45. Read something unrelated but smart . . . pick up a *Harvard Business Review, BusinessWeek, New Yorker, NYT Magazine, Guardian* article.

46. If you don't get something about the project, ask a question. Ask lots of questions. Don't proceed if you're not clear. Question conventional wisdom, even if it means questioning what everyone else says is obvious.

47. Be optimistic. People overrate cynicism and underrate optimism.

48. Have a strong point of view. Provoke people to think beyond standard ideas or break into new territory. Push out of comfort zones and cause some controversy. Piss people off.

49. Create new tools and methods if the old ones don't suit this reality. It makes no sense to keep using a tool just because you've used it in the past. Does it work for this task, today?

50. You belong here. You're exactly where you're supposed to be. All the resources and opportunities you need are already here. Don't sweat it.

amp your
EMPATHY

SIMON KEMP

WE ARE SOCIAL | SINGAPORE

chapter

"Empathy is about finding echoes of another person in yourself."
– Mohsin Hamid

I'd worried about getting exhausted if I scheduled two hosts back to back for the project, so between Hong Kong and Singapore, I took a short vacation on Koh Samui, an island in Thailand. I spent a week relaxing on the beach, exercising every day, and sampling massaman curries at every opportunity.

I arrive in Singapore on a Sunday evening, about as tanned as my fair skin gets, sporting a pink maxi dress. Despite being in a sea of suits and casual wear, I'm not ready to give up my vacation mind-set just yet.

I thought my Dutch residence status might result in my having to pee into a cup at customs—even nonresidents can be forced to take a drug test—but I sail through. I peer out the window of the taxi at the evenly spaced streetlights above. It's already dark, and at first I feel I could be in any large city. The moon casts a glow on the downtown skyscrapers, and then I recognize the iconic Marina Bay Sands, which looks like a huge Roman numeral three. I've heard it's home to the highest and largest rooftop infinity pool in the world. The next twenty minutes pull me forward down a four-lane highway, revealing a sprawling modern city with many more trees than I expected. The landscaping is more deliberate than Hong Kong, which seems carved out of the jungle by comparison.

Simon Kemp, my host, is the managing director of We Are Social Singapore. In business, Asia is arguably the equivalent of the Wild West, and more wild still are social and digital specialty fields within the world of Asian marketing. But Simon, with his Scottish origins, is an unlikely cowboy on both fronts—and I'm Texan, so I know real cowboys.

What makes him a cowboy in my estimation? Well, for starters, he's courageous. When he first came to Asia from London in 2007, he leapt in without a job lined up, following a girl to see what was out here for him and believing that the net would appear. He was also drawn here by the sheer amount of opportunity and his strong drive to experience different cultures. And he's entrepreneurial, as evidenced less than a year ago by his latest venture to start up this office, which specializes in building brands through social channels.

On the other hand, Simon's appearance and mannerisms do not scream cowboy. He's got a thin build and fair skin, and he wears glasses, the sleek metal frames rather than the thick black hipster type. When you meet him, it doesn't take long for him to come back with the most perfect imitation Thai accent in response to something you've said. In fact, he can pull off most voices with masterful skill, like someone playing the piano by ear. And he's a strategic mastermind who has consistently made his ideas tangible and participated in different networks, whether in the form of e-books or trance mixes.

Although Simon and I have known each other for a long time on the Internet, it wasn't until we got on Skype for the first time to discuss this project that he realized I wasn't Dutch. It's time to fill in some of the gaps of our digital personas, and I can't wait to dig into Simon's work and learn how We Are Social approaches social marketing.

The interior of the apartment where Simon and his Singaporean wife, Sarah, live is very modern with an open-plan kitchen, dining room, and living room. There are papers spread across every inch of the dining table around Simon's laptop.

"Pardon the mess," he tells me as he and Sarah give me the grand tour, "but I've been working all day."

The sliding glass door is open to the balcony while a ceiling fan converts the warm night air into a breeze. Simon pulls my suitcase into the guest room, and then he shows me the bathroom and their room.

"And that's the whole east wing," he says. "Now, have you eaten? We were hoping to all go out for supper if that's all right with you?"

"That sounds great."

Next to the apartment building is one of Singapore's famous hawker centers, a large open-air prepared-food market.

"Street food is one of my passions," Simon tells me as he points out his favorite stalls for noodles, curries, coffees, and sugarcane juices there. "The food is one of the top reasons I moved here, honestly. There are centers like this all over the island, something like a hundred or more. The government created them to both stamp out food poisoning and improve social cohesion. Imagine if all of these stalls were street carts instead and how hard it would be to inspect them all and enforce any kind of standard. And how unlikely people would be to sit together and enjoy their meals."

As evidence that opposites attract, Sarah is rather shy and seems more comfortable listening to Simon and me chat. By her own admission she rarely socializes with people she doesn't already know well. Simon, on the other hand, will talk to anyone, which is probably a requirement if you're going to run a social media business.

Because it's a Sunday, many of the stalls are closed. Simon and Sarah order a plate of fried dumplings for us to share and noodle soups all around. They go for beer, and I choose a bright green sugarcane juice served in an oversized clear mug that resembles a barrel with a handle.

I'm excited to eat my way through Simon's Singapore. "What else do you think I should try while I'm here?" I ask.

"Singapore is known for chicken rice. It's quite simple really, just chicken and rice and the juice of the chicken, but it's amazing. Then there are dumplings filled with soup—those are delicious. Oh and I love Thai food at the moment.

"It's not so much a specific dish, though. I think the reality for me is that every day you can have something different. You can go an entire year in Singapore not eating the same food and still having amazing food every day. I do have dishes that I eat three times a week, but that's just because I like to revel in my favorites."

"I'm like that too," I say. "Both with food and my favorite music on repeat. How do you decide which stalls to even try? It seems a little overwhelming."

"It's a bit of a game to crack the mystery of it all. There might be a little old lady at this one stall on the other side of the island that sells one dish, and she'll constantly have a line twenty-people deep, but if you weren't right next to it, you wouldn't even see that stall. You could be on the other side of the same hawker center and you'd not see it. I still discover new places all the time."

I can see what he means as I marvel at the maze-like rows of stalls all wedged together. It's nice that Simon, Sarah, and I share this foodie passion. We carry on discussing the ins and outs of the Singapore food scene all through dinner.

Afterward, back at the apartment, Simon makes sure I have everything I need and demonstrates how to use the air conditioner before heading back to the dining table and his work.

As I lie in bed, my vacation mode melts away, and I begin to imagine going into the office the next morning. I'm very curious to see the inner workings of a social media company.

In the morning, I find Simon at the dining table again. The only indication he's left his post at some point in the night is his change of clothing.

"How did you sleep?" he asks.

"Better than you, I suspect. When did you go to bed?"

"I think two or so. There are so many projects and proposals at the moment. Which is why it's great to have you here to help."

We walk with Sarah to the subway next to the apartment before she parts ways to head off to her own job as a media strategist. Simon and I make one transfer and then emerge at Raffles Place, a funny-sounding name that certainly has nothing to do with games of chance and everything to do with Sir Stamford Raffles, the British statesman who founded the city in 1819 and is now known as the "Father of Singapore."

The landscaping along every street is perfectly manicured, and there isn't a single errant spot of dried gum anywhere. Before I arrived, I'd heard about Singapore's strict laws, such as not allowing the sale of chewing gum anywhere in the country. And it seems that the steep punishments for vandalism like caning have resulted in a much cleaner city.

COMMUNITY ARCHITECTS

We Are Social is hyperaware that people rely on other people to feel a sense of belonging, to make decisions, and simply to get through this thing called life. And they know that all of the tools and platforms a social media company works with are only the means to help people do more of what we are all hardwired to do already, and do it more easily. We Are Social helps brands navigate through this world with a mind to help each and every one be less of a—*ahem*—tosser. (Think of brands that have royally screwed up without We Are Social's guidance, like Kenneth Cole. During the Arab Spring, the corporate giant created a backlash with their poor-taste tweet "Millions are in uproar in #Cairo. Rumor is they heard our new spring collection is now available online.")

Being less than a year old, the Singapore office is small. It's just a room, actually, with desk space for six and not much else. The rest of the team is already seated and busy, but they pause for friendly introductions. Gwen, Simon's second in command, is a Singapore native with a big smile who welcomes me immediately. Dhanuj and Cai Yu, who sit near the window, are a little shyer. Dhanuj is a young upstart, her aura optimistic, and although she's also a local, her accent is English. Cai Yu is fair and has large glasses that take up half her face and enlarge her eyes.

The niceties over, this small team gets cracking on the day's assignments: pulling together a pitch for an Asian beer brand and searching for influencers to help launch a new school. In many ways, these projects could live inside any of the past agencies where I've worked. The difference at We Are Social comes from trying to create communities or conversations for their clients' brands, not just launching messages on their target audiences.

"In this part of the world," Simon tells me, "the majority of potential clients coming in are saying, 'We need a Facebook page with a million fans by next week.' And we respond, 'OK. Really? Why?'"

"Wow," I say. "The discussion starts at the opposite end of the spectrum for the majority of my past clients. Usually they think Facebook and Twitter serve no purpose except to give customers a new way to complain, or they think social media is a free channel for their pushy sales messages. And they don't seem to see how behaving that way totally turns people off."

Simon proudly talks me through the work he and his team have done for the Singapore Standard Chartered Marathon. The client came to them with a Facebook page that had about 17,000 fans. Trouble was, the page was a catchall for complaints.

"What we did was transform the page from a target for any and all discontent about the race into a destination where participants could talk about what they really cared about: running. We became their staff and spent a huge amount of time just talking with people, so answering questions, yes, but also starting conversations around carbo-loading and finding running partners. The page shifted from event-based talk to subject-based talk. It was sort of magical when we'd see people come on to ask a question about something, and the community would answer before we came in for our scheduled check. Or someone might have a rant, but we'd only see the evidence of the community piling in and taking him down a peg. The original person had deleted their whinging before we ever had to do anything. People felt so strongly about the community that it became self-sustaining by the members moderating it themselves. That's what a good community should be." (Read more of Simon's philosophy of community building in *One-Night-Stand Marketing*.)

As Simon shares this case, I realize what's remarkable about building a community. Ultimately the Standard Chartered Marathon *will* be able to sell places in their race, but it's because they have looked outward and identified with the experiences of the runners of Singapore. They have built trust and forged relationships based on the foundation of their community's interests.

REACHING OUR EMPATHY POTENTIAL

Begin searching "social media is making . . . " and Google immediately suggests "social media is making us more social" and "social media is making us antisocial" (not to mention "social media is making you stupid"). Which is it, Google?

On the one hand, if we as a society are constantly chasing link-bait headlines in our newsfeed, shopping for selfie sticks, and chronicling our lives in a self-obsessed manner to boost our fragile feelings, then sure, chalk up a few points for stupider and antisocial. On the other hand, if, as I believe, these tools are helping us stay in touch with people we would otherwise regret having lost contact with, and if they're letting us into the inner lives of others (hopefully, some others very different from ourselves), and giving us a wider perspective on what it means to be human, then social media might be prepping humanity to treat each other and our planet better.

Roman Krznaric is even more of a Pollyanna than I am. In his book *Empathy: Why It Matters, and How to Get It*, he explains how despite possessing "complex brains that are wired for both individualism and empathy," we are only just beginning to understand the power that empathy has to revolutionize society for the better.

Our empathic nature has evolutionary roots, which are observable in other species similar to us. Krznaric details one study where a monkey is offered a choice of reward: either a treat just for himself or a treat for himself and a partner monkey. Once the monkey learned the difference between the two rewards, he preferred the "pro-social" option. Our nearest evolutionary cousins have the capacity to do well by doing good.

The book also taught me that our potential for empathy is not fixed: A school program called Roots of Empathy designed for five- to twelve-year-olds has each classroom "adopt" a baby who visits regularly so students can think about the feelings and perspective of an "other." Studies have proved that teaching such empathic techniques in schools reduces bullying, improves cooperation, and even increases grades.

Knowing that we have this potential makes Obama's rallying cry in his 2006 commencement address at Northwestern University all the more incisive: "There's a lot of talk in this country about the federal deficit. But I think we should talk more about our empathy deficit—our ability to put ourselves in someone else's shoes, to see the world through those who are different from us."

And while Krznaric is very cynical about marketers using empathic techniques that help them understand people only for evil ends—"the marketing industry displays little genuine concern for consumers' welfare" is how he puts it—strategists have been the ones swimming upstream, championing the opposite. I have seen through the eyes of thousands of people because of the research I've had the privilege to be a part of. I've stepped into homes around the world to discover how ice cream or cars fit into family life, the worries people have about their finances, or what it's like to have a child considering military service. My concern with a career focusing solely on social media is that there won't be the same opportunities to experience that depth of understanding of people.

"The funny thing is," Simon says in response to my concerns, "marketers scorn photos of lunch almost as much as photos of kittens and see it as 'proof' that social media is all a waste of time. However, these are the same people that then spend thousands of dollars on research that 'informs' them about their audience—research that often fails to turn up any useful insight. The irony is that we can learn more from looking at photos of people's lunch than we can from 90 percent of all the market research that lands on our desks. I'm not sure how much value you'll take from knowing that 61.7 percent of consumers this month are aged 25 to 34, up 1.3 percent since last month."

I nod. Sometimes it boggles the mind to think how much time we spend looking at numbers out of habit rather than focusing on what is insightful and what changes the way we view our challenges.

Simon continues on his lunch-photo soapbox: "Spending a few minutes a day looking at the photos of your audience's lunch can actually provide amazing insights. Do they eat the same sort of local food every day, or do they like to explore different things? This can help you understand how important regular innovation is to them. Are they health food addicts, or is it a burger every day? For gyms, health-care brands, and governments, this is valuable information. How much are they spending on lunch? Are they willing to spend $15 on a salad? If so, you get a sense of their priorities, and how they determine 'value.' Are they eating alone, or with friends? You get the idea. All of this is amazingly valuable stuff—all just from looking at 'photos of my lunch.'

"By looking at the broad scope of things that people post, we start to get a rich picture of their lives. Sure, that may be the 'curated' version—the life they'd like other people to think they lead—but even that tells you about what's important to them. We may not quite be living it in the same way you would doing ethnography, but social listening allows us to do it at scale—at much lower cost—and still get many of the same benefits. It's also fascinating!"

Personally, I believe Simon is able to draw out so many insights from social listening precisely because he, like me, has been face to face with so many people conducting interviews. This ability to empathize with people, to see patterns, and to glean new understanding about behavior is honed over time to where it's almost like being able to see auras that others can't.

I do love that technology is enhancing or enabling new ways to see inside others' experiences. For example, I've been a member of something called The Listserve (thelistserve.com) for a couple of years now. It's an e-mail lottery where one of the 25,000 members is chosen each day to e-mail the entire list of members. It's a quick daily peek into the life of a student, a patient, or a mother that can be incredibly enlightening. One e-mail from an Illinois woman described her personal experience living with autism, attempting to explain how her experience is much more about sensory overload than the social awkwardness and functional spectrums more frequently discussed. It was touching and fascinating.

So while I have learned things from the digital lives that people create and I see how there will always be further opportunities to learn more, if I had never done the on-ground, in-person work, I think I'd be missing a key component of what it means to be a strategist. I'm biased against strategists whose predominant tool to learn about people is a sentiment analysis.

BUSINESSES DON'T DO VULNERABLE

But listening is only one side of the empathy coin. In his book *Empathy: Why It Matters, and How to Get It*, Krznaric goes into detail on how conversation can build empathy. It requires genuine listening of the kind Simon describes, but it also requires sharing part of yourself with the other person. "Empathy is built on mutual exchange," Krznaric writes.

The Standard Chartered Marathon example is interesting for focusing on the interests of runners first, but I wonder what interaction is like among runners. "So many companies focus only on the listening," I say, "but given We Are Social is a conversation company, how do you help companies hold up their side of the conversation?"

"Well, because we can see when the audience responds well and when they don't," Simon tells me, "there's a feedback loop that guides what we say and what we share next."

So in the same way that I measure my own impact in a conversation in real life, when I see a furrowed brow of confusion, I do respond differently compared to seeing the nod of understanding.

"We've also taken to asking a lot of more fundamental questions on Twitter," he says. "There's nothing like getting feedback from a range of people to help you challenge your perceptions and accepted wisdom, and hopefully come to better answers."

While humbly asking for feedback is a start, I think we've only seen a tiny hint of any sort of vulnerability out of corporations. Many corporate brands tout their intent to be more human in their brand guidelines but do little to prove that they're made up of real humans. On Twitter, the convention to identify who has written the post, such as by adding a tag like "^Heather," is a start. When I worked with Pampers, their social team was made up of parents who could speak on the same level as other parents. They staffed their team properly and did not rely on robots to respond, and they did not lose the plot in online exchanges (to get a taste, research the customer service disasters of brands like American Airlines or Bank of America, for example).

It seems to me that getting the customer service part right should be job one before ever trying to run campaigns. But until the people running the social media channels are able to put themselves in the shoes of their customers, they will always find it challenging to respond well to customer complaints, whether privately over the phone or publicly on social media.

SOCIAL ENGINEERING

My favorite marketing satire takes a huge dig at social media. Writer and associate creative director E.B. Davis equally delighted and mortified the people of adland with his Tumblr called "Things Real People Don't Say About Advertising." He took simple stock photos of people and memed them up with incisive headlines. One shows a guy in a suit in front of his laptop, fists clenched in extreme enthusiasm, with the line "FUCK YEAH I'LL JOIN THE CONVERSATION!!!!!!!!!!!!!" (Yes, I did fact-check the number of exclamation marks.) Another shows a pensive older gentleman with a thought bubble that reads "I wonder if my favorite brand of kitchen roll has a Twitter stream I can follow?"

I've been in too many meetings where clients acted as though we live in a parallel universe where people *actually* feel this way.

The thought leader, Marcus Collins, Executive Director of Social Engagement at Doner in Detroit, has also made it his business to counter such delusional beliefs. He defiantly speaks out for good social media management, which he labels *social engineering*. Instead of the more sinister usage of the phrase where someone hijacks your identity, he uses the term to define the building blocks a brand ought to adhere to when using social tools: "Give people a reason to tell a story, help them strengthen the relationships they already have, and create opportunities for people to connect with new people."

Good customer service aligns with Collins' beliefs because those positive experiences can give a person a reason to tell a story. One of my favorite examples is Netflix. They've been known to lighten the mood with *Star Trek*–themed online chats: "This is Cpt. Mike of the good ship Netflix. Which member of the crew am I speaking with today?"

One especially steamy afternoon, Simon, Gwen, Dhanuj, Cai Yu, and I eat lunch at a hawker center close to the office to sample the chicken rice. Gwen demonstrates how you save a table by placing a pack of tissues at an open seat. Then, as we stand in line together, I share Collins's beliefs about social engineering with Simon.

"If we want people to tell stories," he tells me, "we have to realize they'll be most interested in stories about themselves, not about our brands. They're the protagonists; we're just the support cast. I think Red Bull is a perfect example. They don't just sponsor a person; they fund that person's quest for their dreams and personal achievement. It's always about how that person has stretched themselves, not how Red Bull is the hero."

This immediately brings to mind for me Red Bull's Stratos stunt, where they sponsored Felix Baumgartner to skydive from the stratosphere.

Unbelievable content certainly gets spread, but so too does useful content that provides practical value. Tips such as the ones posted by the Standard Chartered Marathon about how to approach carbo-loading are supremely useful to their community and are frequently passed along further by their fans. Similarly, the We Are Social team puts together lots of great reports on the digital landscape in Asia, and these are full of helpful tips on how to utilize social media.

"Giving away useful content has been a powerful way for us to build our business," Simon had told me when I first arrived and expressed shock at the number of proposals they were putting together.

A brand can also think about creating experiences that bring customers closer to their own networks of people. For example, Ticketmaster has a simple tool when buying tickets that lets you see if any of your friends are also attending an event, so you can then choose to sit near them. And Simon taught me that, according to Twitter, Super Bowl commercials that include a hashtag get mentioned 60 percent more than those that don't. That's such a little thing to aid in creating a conversation.

Finally, brands that practice social engineering can help people find new people who might be like-minded. For example, I've had fantastic experiences with Airbnb. Their social graph overlay identifies people who are a degree of separation away in your social network. That's how I ended up spending a weekend staying in the London apartment of a strategist I didn't know the last time I visited.

One evening, Simon and I take the metro home, and he tells me about Story Sync. "It's this great little second-screen app that AMC [the channel that brought us *Breaking Bad* and *The Walking Dead,* among others] has with quizzes and insight about your favorite TV shows. When people are watching TV and using their phones, tablets, or laptops, 75 percent of the time it has nothing to do with the show. But with this app, people can participate with others who are watching the same show they are and get a real-time experience."

Overall, Simon's insights have taught me to be very suspicious of brands' propensity toward self-interest when it comes to social media. Social media works best when it's used as a tool to help people do more of what they really want to do, so if we're going to use this technology to try to influence behavior in the service of brands, we need to better understand the networks that people are creating and care more about those individuals than we care about our brand. And that's what so many brands get totally wrong. As we work to build brands, the best thing we can do is amplify our empathy for other people.

THE SEARCH FOR DRIER ISLANDS

On Saturday, I leave Simon to continue his workaholic ways at his dining table to meet up with Alex Marquez, founder of innovation consultancy, Propellerfish. When I was a grad student at the University of Texas, I taught a supplemental lab for a very large introduction to advertising class, and Alex was one of my students. He went on to work at brand and innovation consultancy What If?! in New York, and then he started his own business here in Singapore. Alex is an all-American-looking guy, married to a German gal who chose Singapore to work on her PhD. He's enthusiastic and quite worldly. I never fail to learn something whenever we get the chance to reconnect.

We'd agreed to meet at a small patisserie called Kki Sweets. The little shop sells beautiful cakes and, off to the side, gifts and stationery. The aesthetic is Japanese Nostalgic: woven among the new items are endless shelves of Polaroid cameras, manual pencil sharpeners, and old magazines—perhaps it's more Hoarder Chic.

I tuck into a passion fruit-coconut mousse so light and perfectly sweet that an Asian stereotype emerges in my mind: I didn't think Asians really did dessert? Alex goes for a glossy chocolate mousse with a raspberry center and one perfect raspberry perched on top of the tiny cylinder.

It's so easy for Americans to talk about work, so we do. We begin by discussing the relative pros and cons of focusing your energies on general advertising or social or innovation.

"I think the choice of what you do with your time is really critical," he tells me. "Advertising agencies are kind of like the Maldives. Have you heard what's happening there?"

"All I know is that it's supposed to be a brilliant place to scuba dive," I say, remembering reading about these islands on every must-see-before-you-die list.

"Well," Alex says. "scientists are predicting that in fifty to one hundred years, global warming will melt the ice caps, and these islands are so near sea level that they'll be swallowed up. It's pretty interesting because after trying to raise international awareness of the problem to lower carbon emissions and save the islands, the most recent president looked into relocating the entire country's population. His idea was to purchase land in Australia or Sri Lanka or India and move over two hundred and fifty thousand people to a new home."

"Jeez, I had no idea," I say. But it makes sense: Global warming is going to ruin a lot of beautiful places. "It's hard to even imagine a problem so big that the most pragmatic solution is to relocate all those people."

"Yeah, and I think it's the perfect parallel to what's going on in advertising."

My brain grabs onto this idea. The blatant failing to embrace change among advertising agencies and marketing consultancies has been labeled as our "Kodak moment" by Gareth Kay, co-founder of consultancy Chapter. But perhaps it's really our Maldivian moment.

Overall, most companies have reacted to these struggles by diversifying their offerings. It's common these days to see any combination of consulting, data analytics, product innovation, advertising, media planning, public relations, and internal communications under one roof. Ad agencies sometimes come up with new products. Media agencies have ad ideas. Innovation firms uncover human insights that redefine a brand. This is creating conflict among companies, especially when they're asked to work together on "loop" teams. No one ever keeps anyone in the loop in my experience.

That's because there's always more budget to be commandeered. Agencies play nice in front of the clients, but get an account handler alone with his client and the conversation turns to all the other things his company could be doing and how his agency needs to "get to the table" earlier in the process.

Clients think they're buying best-in-class services when they cobble together these teams, but I think loop teams are dangerous. One of my favorite examples of smart work is a campaign Canon did in Australia. They created an idea they call *photochains*, which is essentially an inspiration game housed on a microsite. They kicked it off with several example chains: In each photo, a detail was highlighted to inspire the next photo in the chain. So, say there was a picture of a child with an orange wedge in his smiling mouth, and the photographer selects the orange. This means the next photo has to have something to do with orange, which could be an alleyway in Spain with an orange door. That photographer might highlight and suggest "door" for the following photographer, and so on.

What's beautiful about this idea is that I don't believe it could have been created in a loop team. If Canon's above-the-line agency of record (primarily tasked with TV creation) started working against a brief to inspire people to take more pictures, it's very unlikely that they'd present a digital platform as the crux of their idea. This particular idea uses above-the-line TV and outdoor to build awareness of and drive people to the site.

From my past experience, working on large brands as the "digital" agency partner among many other communications companies on a loop team was, at times, insanely frustrating. The TV idea was expected to be created and approved first, followed by a cascade of other channels that expressed the idea from TV. Trouble is, communications are not linear, and ideas are not widgets efficiently constructed on an assembly line.

Instead, ideas *can* be like solar flares and emanate from any medium. To come up with ideas that work in a post-digital world, it's better, I think, to concept there first. CP+B would handle this by sometimes mandating that the first round of work shown to the creative directors could not have TV ideas. That worked well. By contrast, the worst process is when the above-the-line agency sells in a TV script, and then the digital agency has to "make it participatory." That's when you know you're in for several painful rounds, and you most want to join those Maldivians and move elsewhere. Or just drown.

Other client corporations are responding to the changing communications landscape by taking the creative thinking formerly done by an agency in-house. Red Bull and Burberry are examples of established companies that don't really use ad agencies. Start-ups like Uber and Slack have also grown through their own in-house marketing efforts. Many recent grads would rather work for these types of companies where they get to apply their thinking toward changing the product and the experience rather than standing behind a figurative bullhorn barking marketing messages at people. When no one wants to work for Kodak or live on the Maldives, what happens next?

WELCOME TO THE VIRTUAL ISLAND

Simon had to work all weekend, but on Monday we reconnect to be a part of a Hyper Island Digital Acceleration Master Class. I was invited to speak and suggested to the organizers that Simon speak as well. My plan is to continue teaching these immersive courses on a freelance basis in between the trips for the book.

We ride in a taxi to the venue. Singapore has one of the highest population densities in the world, yet sharing this space with all these people are many trees along the roadways. The greenness is also varied—there are palms, pines, and archetypal, round-topped deciduous trees. We land at our appointed destination on Scotts Road. The small parking lot is flanked by a hotel, bar, restaurant, and the meeting space we are looking for.

The feeling is something like a support group, with the client-side marketers, agency CEOs, managing directors, creative directors, and strategy directors from Singapore as well as from Kuala Lumpur, Hong Kong, and Australia, all here to learn and share their own experiences transitioning to a post-digital world of work and life. Their chairs are set in a U facing the front, and Simon and I sit in the back of the room and observe until it's our turn to speak.

Mark Comerford, who's been in journalism for over twenty years and who once helped put the Swedish government online when there were only five websites out there, takes the stage. The first thing I notice is he's not wearing any shoes. He addresses this right away and tells us he's superstitious and can only present barefoot. He also reads to us from a Lonely Planet guide, which reveals that he and his countrymen from Ireland are known to pepper their speech with profanity so we ought not take offense at that either.

He begins his session by challenging the conventional thinking in the room, and not just on the many possible uses of the word "fuck." He asks for everyone's definition of "digital." The participants dutifully scratch and scribble in their notebooks. Then they read their answers:

"Information that can be broken up into numerical sequences, which makes it easier and much faster to store, copy, and share."

"The Internet."

"New way of communication."

"Connection."

"New business models."

"Can you see a pattern?" Mark asks.

Silence.

"No? Me either. We think we're all talking about the same thing, but we're not. The word 'digital' is more of a problem than a solution. Forget digital for a moment. Try 'network.' Does that change the way we think about what we do? It's an action instead of a label. It's not about the tools; it's about the interactions."

He talks about the change we're experiencing, but he puts it in context. "Think about walking up to someone during the Industrial Revolution and asking them 'What's it like to be a part of the Industrial Revolution?' To them, there's no difference between today and last week, and there's only a little change between today and last year. It's hard to see change when you're in the middle of it."

I love the way Mark tells stories and weaves together his examples with expletives. "Think about growing a potato," he says. "You might say, 'I grew this potato.' But you didn't actually grow the fucking potato. You can't create a community or a conversation just like you can't grow a potato. But you can create the right environment."

I find myself nodding because this is a perfect articulation of what I feel clients so often don't really understand. They see digital as simply another channel—just another method to get their messages out there. But, with respect to the many lovely clients I've worked with who think this way, they are missing out. The thing is, they won't have a network ready when they need one, because their brands are too busy being the drunk at the party, too busy talking about himself rather than being the generous, funny host that no one can get enough of.

The day continues with speakers and exercises. Notebooks get filled with profound ideas, and the ideas stick because the sessions build in time for reflection and for getting the participants to apply these new ways of thinking.

When it's Simon's turn, he shares an eye-opening state of the fast-moving adoption of various technologies in Asia. He has this great way of bringing stats to life.

"Would you believe," he says, "that the number of mobile phones is outpacing toilets and toothbrushes?"

One of the most intriguing discussions revolves around the number of personas the typical Chinese teenager creates. With intense pressure on young people to do well in school, they end up spending a lot of time alone in their rooms (presumably studying). As a result, the average teen creates five different profiles across their social media platforms: the fun self for friends, the polite self for family, the academic self for school, the real self, and the fantasy self. That's a lot of identities to maintain!

The next day I talk to the group about my views on the evolution of brands and communications through three metaphors. First is Brand as a Battleship.

Much of the language we use in marketing, still to this day, is militaristic; for example, a brand "launches" a "campaign" on a "target" audience. But given that people are more in control of obtaining information about products and services through online reviews and corporate websites, the amount of attention paid to advertising has plummeted. (To learn more, look up the *Harvard Business Review* article "The Rising Cost of Consumer Attention" by Thales S. Teixeira.) This lack of attention means it's much more expensive to be militaristic today.

The next metaphor is Brand as a Game Show Host. These brands create imaginary worlds to instigate involvement, because their way of thinking is driven by an obsession with participation and engagement. Think "Upload a picture to win!" But more often than not, the interactions are just gimmicks, and they don't build a story about the brand or a network held together by mutual interests.

My provocation is that brands ought to take door number three: Brand as a Gardener. A gardener creates something of value, but he respects that he can't always predict what will thrive and what will wither. He creates the right environment for a living thing to grow (growing a brand is like growing a fucking potato, remember?). Creating that environment requires an empathic understanding of real people and of what will be useful and entertaining to them. That's the way we ought to look at creating content to build brands.

For example, most gardens have benches and spaces for people to simply enjoy. These gardens make room for others, which is a good parallel to brands like Dell. They've turned their business around simply by taking feedback onboard though their idea submission platform IdeaStorm, which is like a fancy digital suggestion box for improvements.

Over another great dinner of exquisite Chinese food, Simon and I talk about the day.

"I love the gardener metaphor," he says, "and how you brought in great examples of brands behaving like one."

"I thought I might have stretched the gardening conceit a little too far," I say.

"I think it's fun," he says. "Doing cool shit trumps saying shit in a cool way every time. We might never have met if it weren't for you doing something cool with the survey." He waves his chopsticks in my direction. "And we certainly wouldn't be sitting here if I hadn't heard about your project there."

Simon was the only person who responded to my mention of this book idea in the concluding thoughts of the survey. He sent me an e-mail and invited me to come work with him. I'm certain the survey is why people were at least open to consider hosting me for this project: I'd created something of value for them first.

Simon has had a similar experience reaching people through content he's created, but instead of a survey, it was music. He's been in love with electronic music, trance in particular, since he was ten.

"I made mixes in my bedroom, played them to my three friends, and that was as good as it was ever going to get," he told me. "I never had any illusions that I'd be some world-renowned DJ or anything."

Fast-forward to his thirties, in the midst of his advertising career, when he had several clients who were very slow to implement his digital and social media recommendations. "They were spending millions on TV advertising, but they couldn't see why they might be on Facebook."

One night, he was commiserating with colleagues over some drinks and sharing his frustrations, when they challenged him to go out and prove that he could promote something successfully on his own. That very day, he went home and started publishing his mixes. He began promoting them with Facebook ads. He put in five dollars to start. "I uploaded a few mixes and thought, *Let's see what happens*. I woke up the next morning and I had one thousand fans. I thought, *How is this even possible?* I spent another five dollars, and another. I probably put a total of five thousand, and a burgeoning community emerged. People were connecting with me from all over the world. It was an amazing opportunity to meet different people." (Read about one of the more unique people he met through music in *The Broccoli Story*.)

Simon and I both found the process of creating content, and a community around that content, fascinating. And for him, his actions offered real, credible proof he could show to his clients. He had over one hundred thousand Facebook fans. Clients began to listen.

HANG ONTO YOUR EMPATHY

On the Friday before I leave for Amsterdam, Simon and I find time for a drink and a little reflection on our two weeks together. We head around the corner from the office to The Bank, named after the proliferation of financial institutions nearby. We pull up stools at a hightop table on outdoor terrace and order ice-cold drinks to combat the sticky evening.

"So Simon, we're at the end. What's your top tip that I should remember about working with social?" I ask him.

"Hmmm . . . " He thinks for a minute and takes a sip of his beer. "Well, just that people aren't fools. They see through brand bravado and propaganda. And when the emperor is naked, it doesn't take long for the news to spread.

"We've partnered with the World Federation of Advertisers to support their

Project Reconnect. The idea is to encourage all marketers to listen to what people really want from brands and marketing. The idea is to provoke practitioners to take John Willshire's missive to heart: Making things people want is greater than making people want things."

After my two weeks in Singapore, I wonder if there's a place where no one is under any illusion of emperor's clothes. That's where I want to be, and I feel emboldened by this trip to find it.

ONE-NIGHT-STAND
marketing

BY SIMON KEMP

Is your brand a bit slutty? I hate to be the one to tell you this, but think about it. Is your brand focused on transactional relationships? Does it speak in pick-up lines (otherwise known as key messages)? Is it mostly interested in instant gratification at the expense of a more meaningful, enduring relationship?

If your marketing efforts could be characterized this way, it's time to be honest with yourself. Take a hard look at what your brand puts into the world, whether it's your product, your packaging, your advertising, anything about the experience, really. Will anyone actually care?

If you are creating value, they will. That means creating utility or entertainment. Full stop. It does not mean arrogantly assuming that you have more to teach your audience about your brand than you might learn from your audience in return.

Because, as humans, our choices are social. We are far less rational than many business strategy documents would have you believe. We are not individual agents. We are embedded in our communities. As a result, real conversation between people is one of the most important factors in determining our brand choices.

A brand worth talking about is a brand that people are willing to pay more for. And everything a brand does is an opportunity to start a conversation. The packaging. An event. An ad. It takes skill to build a brand worth talking about, where these conversations are positive and people become media.

the BROCCOLI story

BY SIMON KEMP

I'd finished a mix a couple days before. And on a Saturday morning, what I'd normally do is try and gauge the weekend crowd. So I'm on Facebook by about 11:00 a.m., going around different communities and posting the mix to promote it. As a result, I used to get fairly regular friend requests from people I'd never met. They'd come in from all sorts of random people from the other side of the world.

That morning, one popped up from this person called Singgih. I accepted anybody at that time. I didn't really give it a second thought; I just accepted him. Pretty much instantaneously, there was this little bit at the bottom of the screen where the chat messages used to pop up, and he messaged me to say, "Hey, thanks for accepting. How are you?"

We started chatting, and I asked, "Where are you from?"

He said, "Indonesia."

"Oh cool, so what are you doing?"

"I'm in my field planting broccoli."

"What?" I typed back. This was a new one for me.

"Yeah, I used to be a motorcycle mechanic, but I got bored with that lifestyle, and I didn't really think it was right for me, so my wife and I moved to the countryside. Now I'm a broccoli farmer."

He was out in the field, on his phone, planting broccoli, listening to the mix, and chatting to me on Facebook chat on his phone. Out of nowhere there's this kid, early twenties, who had become a farmer but was still listening to techno in his field, and talking to me on Facebook. It was the oddest thing.

And we've carried on talking here and there. He's since given up being a farmer. His wife got bored with the countryside. They've moved back to the city, and he's doing some kind of professional job. That incident made me realize the whole power of what words and content can do to connect people. I'm a Scottish guy who loves techno music, and I can find people to share that love with anywhere. I suppose that's one of the reasons I fell in love with the idea of doing social strategy specifically. What I do doesn't feel like advertising. It feels like I'm building communities with thousands of connections just like the one between the broccoli farmer and me.

practice
ZEN

rOobin GOLESTAN

DMG | Beijing

chapter
THREE

> **"Nothing gives one person so much advantage over another as to remain always cool and unruffled under all circumstances."**
>
> – Thomas Jefferson

The Funk*Fever party in the fifth-floor rooftop lounge at Migas could just as easily be in Dubai or Miami as Beijing. My ears are full of high-decibel disco and classic hip hop courtesy of the DJ who's also my host, rOobin Golestan. The place is brimming with a medley of international partygoers sipping colorful drinks. A pair of massive white egg seats are stuffed with people laughing and chatting beneath an art installation hovering above us all: a glowing red tulip. Or is it a fork? Beijing's air tonight is unusually clear, so when I look over the railing, I can easily see a broad stretch of buildings in the middle distance and Friday night traffic crawling beneath a full moon.

rOobin (who, to avoid being called Robin, opts for phonetic insurance by always writing his name "rOobin") is a true third-culture kid. His parents are Iranian, so he grew up speaking Persian at home even though he was raised in Germany. A chance to work as a strategist on Nike leading up to the Beijing Olympics brought him here to work at DMG, a rather atypical ad agency. Of the myriad nationalities rOobin could meet in Beijing, he managed to meet and fall in love with a fellow German, Katrin, who works as an account director at another agency. Now they have two children: Leo, three, and Henry, ten months.

With a sort of Jedi-mind manner, rOobin mesmerized me on our Skype-call introduction as he described his experiences and ways of thinking. Our conversation hinted at what I might learn from him in Beijing: the importance of practicing a Zen state, even if it might not come as naturally for me as it does for him.

It's a serious business advantage to have a "mind like water," as the martial arts discipline calls this state of perfect readiness, where one is flexible and in possession of a clear mind. But if it were easy, we wouldn't need lessons to achieve it.

rOobin's can't-miss-it Afro bobs up and down behind the decks at the Funk*Fever party, and the A-Team theme song leads into another track. I'm enjoying getting to know Katrin, as well as their friends, a German couple, Birte and Dominic, who live locally, and rOobin's childhood best friend visiting from Germany, Christian. The group has already burst my stereotypical expectations of Germans. They're expressive and laugh loudly. The guys decide to throw back espresso martinis on top of the rosé and spicy foods we'd eaten earlier. That doesn't seem rational. Or wise.

As the singletons, Christian and I talk a bit more. He's not so comfortable with his English, so we mix in a little Spanish, too. He lived in Spain for a while, and now he's a teacher for kids with learning disabilities. A gentle giant. And funny. Did I mention tall? Too bad he has a girlfriend back in Germany.

After rOobin's set, he joins Christian and Dominic, and they start square dancing. Perhaps it's because Dom is wearing cowboy boots that I'm not entirely sure this is really happening. The phones come out; picture after picture is taken. The sky and the dancers begin to spin.

I wake up in a bare corporate apartment with my mouth dry and my eyes straining against the bright light of day. This is one of the first times in a long time that I barely remember getting home. I'm not staying with rOobin on this trip because his place is full of children, and they already have a houseguest. My throbbing head is thankful.

"I feel broken," I tell rOobin over the phone.

"Let's write off today and meet up tomorrow," he says.

WHY CHINA?

After my headache subsides, I muster up some energy and leave the apartment in search of food. This neighborhood is home to DMG, where rOobin works, and is only about fifteen minutes from his home. On my search, I discover several strange shopping centers. One is a sparse, airy building with shops manned by Russian salespeople offering mostly thigh-high boots and platform shoes, but there's no food to be found. Another is a dark, cramped market filled with stall after stall of cleaning supplies and other household necessities. No food there, either. My third try is a success: an American-style mall where I find a place that sells noodles. Nourished but still running low on energy, I retreat from my three-mall adventure back to base to hide from the bright light and loud street noise.

The next day, I meet rOobin, Katrin, the boys, and Christian at "Optical City," a mall comprised of some two hundred small shops spread over four floors, all selling eyeglasses. Katrin, who's looking for a new pair of glasses, maneuvers a stroller through a mob of people, shuttling Leo in front of her while the rest of us follow behind. rOobin is carrying Henry in a sling on his chest.

Katrin, who is somehow able to navigate us through all the identical shops, leads us to a particular stall, picks out what she wants, and begins negotiations with the shop owner, who communicates to her via a large-button calculator.

While we wait for her new glasses to be made, we head outside to a nearby market selling antiques and home décor. It's looks like an open-air hangar, except with endless rows of Buddha statues and gilded lion door knockers. I notice several Chinese men have their T-shirts rolled up, proudly exposing their big bellies.

"Beijing air-conditioning," rOobin tells me, and I get him and Christian to roll up their own shirts for a picture.

After Katrin collects her newly made spectacles, we head off to a café to meet Birte and Dominic for a Yunnan-style lunch. In the US and Europe, I was used to "Chinese" as a single category of food, perhaps with the sub-specifications of "Szechuan" or "dim sum," but here, an entire new world of food awaits me under the umbrella of "Chinese food."

Once we're seated at a table, I ask the Germans, "Why China?"

"It's a happening place," rOobin explains. "It's very dynamic. Not just because we have almost one point four billion people, but because it's changing. It's not the same as it was two years ago, and I hope it won't be the same two years from now. When I got the job offer to come here, I thought it was something I would regret if I didn't take it. The job turned out to be far more challenging and interesting than I ever thought it would be."

Birte, who works as a teacher, adds, "People who grew up in China find it tough to think very long term. It's like having lived in six different eras with how fast things have changed here. People don't expect things to stay the same. They don't take the status quo for granted or try to protect it like we do in Germany. I think it keeps things interesting."

Like Simon had told me, you can always confound people with the numbers for an Asian country, but China's numbers are certainly the most impressive in terms of sheer size. More than one billion people who all identify with a shared idea of country is too hard to imagine. The entire population of the Netherlands is less than that of Beijing alone. There are twenty-five mega cities across China you've probably never heard of, with populations ranging between 2.5 and 10 million people. Chicago has a population of about 2.7 million, but have you ever heard of Harbin, Hefei, or Zibo? They're all larger.

With almost every edition of *The Economist* suggesting that the fast-moving future rests in China's hands, I must consider moving here—at least, if I want to catch a ride to that future.

FUTURE FOCUSED

Something is different on this leg of my journey: rOobin has recently quit his job, so he's invited me to witness his last two weeks as head of strategy for DMG. He doesn't have a new job lined up, and that's intentional as he's planning to take some time to be with the boys and Katrin, then to take a trip with his two best guy friends before exploring what his next job move should be.

rOobin has been with DMG for just short of five years. DMG is not just an ad agency; rather, it owns an ad agency (and a production company and a feature-film business). It's an important distinction built on an obvious idea that most ad agencies forget: Advertising isn't the center of the universe.

Twenty years ago, CEO Dan Mintz and his two Chinese partners, Wu Bing and Peter Xiao, started the company as an ad-production firm. DMG made a natural progression into an integrated agency, but its evolution really took a major step when they crossed the chasm into film production and distribution and learned to generate creative content that people are willing to pay for.

This transition happened right around the time of the Beijing Olympics, which marked a pivotal moment in China's history. The Olympics were an invitation to the world to see China take center stage. China was on the rise regardless, but the Olympics acted as a catalyst for even more rapid change. In the film industry, for example, China crossed the threshold of five thousand theater screens across the country soon after the Olympics ended. Prior to 2012, only twenty films from outside of China could be imported per year (that number is now thirty-four). When you think of the number of people in the country, you realize that each one of those twenty films therefore amounts to millions if not billions of dollars in ticket sales.

But it's not only Chinese films that can be distributed freely. If your film is acknowledged as a Chinese co-production, it's possible to skirt the twenty-film limit. Such a designation requires a Chinese investor and Chinese actors playing main characters, and for the shooting to take place at least partly in China. Oh, and it must represent the country in an approved manner.

This is the landscape DMG is navigating by co-investing and co-producing films. Two of their most notable projects, *Looper* and *Iron Man 3*, incorporated an understanding of both Western and Chinese culture to create not only coherent but undoubtedly entertaining plots and themes. For example, *Looper* has a memorable scene between Joseph Gordon-Levitt and Jeff Daniels where Gordon-Levitt has a plan to get out of the hitman business and run off to France. Daniels's character reproaches, "I'm from the future. You should go to China." That's the kind of positive, yet truthful, reframing China is looking to export to the rest of the world.

This marriage of the film business and the ad business within one company has developed new strengths among DMG staff. First off, what creative person doesn't have a half-finished screenplay in a drawer? It makes it easier to recruit people when you can offer projects on both advertising and film. But more than that, these two worlds cross-pollinate within their walls: DMG employees believe that they create better branded content as a result of their expertise in film.

So why would rOobin leave?

"I've loved being able to work across film and advertising, and even advertising for films," rOobin tells me over coffee in the mall across the street from the office. "But you can't have time; you have to take time. That's what it's come down to for me. I want to take time for things I don't have enough time for: meeting friends, traveling, spending time with the kids and with my parents, and working on creative projects like DJing. I want to only take on interesting and short freelance projects, so I'm in control of my time."

It's a theme I'm hearing more and more. Before coming to Beijing, I had a Skype conversation with another strategist in the US, Heidi Hackemer. After coming up through the ranks at DraftFCB, Fallon London, and BBH New York, Heidi realized that to do her best work and get her best ideas, she needed to make sure she took time away from the job to draw inspiration from other environments and situations. "All my inputs were coming from Twitter feeds and Mintel reports," she said.

So she bought a big black truck and oscillated between exploring America and freelancing with different clients. She went to volunteer in post-flood Virginia, she camped in the desert, and she worked on a dude ranch, but she also applied her brain to brands in between trips.

"I really love brands and strategy," she told me. "I wanted to figure out how I could honor this discipline I love and do what I'm meant to do: bring in fresh air and divergent thinking. I really love people and ideas. The traveling is making me so much better at my job. I'm more interesting, and now I understand real people."

Heidi has since started her own company, Wolf & Wilhelmine, based on this more humane and inspiration-inducing way of working. She's a delightful, extreme optimist, and she's also really clear on her mission: She has no desire to be on stage at Cannes; rather, she wants to inspire those people. But she's come to realize that to be inspiring, she needs space. She needs to allow her mind to wander. This makes her a big proponent of boredom: "Boredom is essential for creativity."

rOobin and I talk about the welcome potential boredom that's ahead for him, and it's like I'm from the future, living a Thoreau-esque sabbatical and encouraging rOobin's choice. It's just unfortunate that the ad industry doesn't allow for boredom. The US goes too far with its "always-on" mentality, where sabbaticals are the exception. I feel like Europe knows how to keep things a little more sane. There's no guilt around taking holiday time like there is in the US. But no matter where you are, fully unplugging from your responsibilities takes a few months, and most full-time jobs won't permit such sabbaticals.

"You have to see this TED talk that Stefan Sagmeister did," I tell rOobin. "He closes his design studio every seventh year and says that, on a scale of one to ten in terms of importance to replenishing creativity, these sabbaticals rate a twelve."

"It's a shame companies don't just offer sabbaticals," rOobin replies, "but I'm ready for the next thing anyway. It's hard to keep learning at the same place. At some point, you deeply understand the people, the clients, the ways of working. Changing those aspects will probably result in just as much learning as the time off."

ZEN STRATEGY

Somehow, rOobin effortlessly travels between the more serious tasks of going to work and taking care of the kids toward the more lighthearted nights with friends and DJing on rooftops. His nature is even keel. I'm finding that rOobin is more than just someone who can easily switch gears; he's a guy who has harnessed his natural ability to keep things in perspective at all times. There is calmness about him. He speaks more slowly than most people. He's not a control freak, but he's always in control: of his speaking, his easy smile, and his presence. This has no doubt helped him in his work and is what I most hope to steal from him.

After work, we hop on his electric scooter for a ride around town. We pass one of the few preserved city gates from the wall around the city, which has mostly been removed. The corners of the roof curl up in the quintessential style of ancient Chinese architecture. The buildings around us block the late afternoon sun, and exhaust fumes and the bitterness of pollution linger in my nose. Green and orange taxis and commuters crowd the streets, but we weave through and around them, honking.

The honking, rOobin tells me, is "Beijing brakes."

We arrive at rOobin's apartment complex: The buildings are connected with glass-enclosed pathways that look like arms stretching shoulder to shoulder. It's a fairly new and ecologically minded place to live. Using geothermal wells, the complex taps the earth's below-the-surface constant temperature, which is unaffected by the season. This system naturally cools the buildings in the summer and heats them in the winter.

After eating and putting the boys to bed, rOobin, Christian, and I share a bottle of wine outside, where the buildings circle reflecting ponds full of koi. There are a few patio-type swings built to seat four people, consisting of two swings joined together and facing each other with a table in between. We sit in the warm night air, drinking from plastic cups.

"Who would you most want to meet, living or dead?" rOobin asks.

I think about it and rattle off Mark Twain and the founder of LinkedIn, Reid Hoffman. "Reid could probably introduce me to some really interesting people," I reason.

rOobin's choice of Socrates reflects his preference to ponder what is important in life and his ability to take time for what matters. Christian most wants to meet Che Guevara. I had no clue he was so idealistic, but, I think, perhaps it makes sense, given his role working with special needs children.

"What superhero power would you wish for?" I ask.

rOobin wants to time travel, and Christian wants a quick wit in all situations. I tell them I'd want to be able to speak all languages.

We watch tiny bugs skim the water. The guys start discussing their upcoming travel plans to the Taklamakan Desert in Northwest China with another childhood friend, Martin.

rOobin tells me about a German saying: "Friends are the ones you make before twenty-five. Acquaintances come after."

Since we're both over thirty, I hope that saying is wrong.

It's nice to just banter, but my mind turns to the purpose of my visit. I change the subject to strengths and weaknesses in our characters, hoping to learn more about rOobin while Christian is there to confirm or deny.

rOobin offers up his weaknesses first: "Maybe I embrace the position of the devil's advocate a little too much," he says. "I can challenge people in a confronting way. I feel you have a more winning way of doing that, Heather—a bit more of a charming way. Maybe it's just your personality. But it is indeed more difficult to be opposed to a positively articulated argument than a confronting, challenging one."

I tell rOobin I think his greatest strength is his really Zen nature. He's unflappable. I can't imagine him angry.

"You have this firm grasp on perspective," I tell him, "like you know things will happen when it's time for them to happen. I don't think many people are able to live this philosophy like you do."

He refills his cup. "I believe in something John Lennon said: 'Life is what happens to you while you're busy making other plans.' I didn't foresee where I am a year ago, and I definitely didn't think I'd stay in China for more than five years. Seven years ago, I never imagined ever moving to China. Probably and hopefully life is going to continue to surprise me."

"So how do you see that attitude come to life when you're at work?" I ask.

"I think I'm more accepting of whatever happens that's outside of my control. Like, if I've traveled out of town for a meeting and it gets canceled moments before it's meant to start. That is not uncommon in China. And I've found that the best way to deal with constant change is simply to be proactive. You can control your effort, and how productive you are with it, even if you can't control the outcome. What keeps us from being Zen is expectations. The moment you expect certain things, chances are good you won't get exactly that."

I turn to Christian. "Do you see this Zen attitude in rOobin, too?"

"rOobin has *gelassenheit*," he replies.

"What does that mean?"

"It basically means calmness," rOobin answers for him. "Um, serenity or tranquility, I guess. We use it more in German than you'd use the English words."

"So where does that come from?" I ask. "Were you just born with it?"

"I don't think it's only that," he says. "When I first started working, I met up with an old friend I'd studied with, and I was having a bit of a rant about the long hours and hard work in the ad agency. Then she told me she just had a patient who had committed suicide. And there was an awkward silence after that. What we're working on might be worth millions, but it's not life and death. It's always good to put things into perspective and remind ourselves of that."

"To me, you don't need to put things into perspective because they're always in perspective for you," I say.

"I've never thought about it like that," he responds, "but now that we're talking about it, I know I've had many colleagues who I thought to myself, *Why are you fighting this? Why are you not putting this into perspective? This is just who you're dealing with.*"

rOobin and I both enjoy working with Zen people, even though this type is rarer in this business.

"There's this book *What Color Is Your Parachute?*," I say. "It's one of those self-helpy, figure-out-what-career-is-best-for-you books. I thought it was interesting because in addition to choosing based on your interests, it also suggests choosing a career based on the types of people who tend to be drawn to the type of work. This business probably attracts fewer Zen people than any other type. With the creativity comes instability or aggression.

"So if we want more Zen, we may just have to start our own agency . . . and you'll have to teach me your ways."

"You're already pretty Zen to me," he says, "and I think I know why." He pauses for several beats.

"Tell me, Zen master!" I say.

"It's because you're good at reading people. If you're able to read people, it's easier to put the situation into perspective, because you understand why they might be passionate about certain things or why they're frustrated. Then it's easier not to fight them, because you realize they're not fighting you; they're fighting themselves and their own expectations."

For me, observing someone like rOobin who approaches life with such a Zen nature is inspiring. Personally, I don't think I am where I want to be yet, and I know how frustrated I can become when I'm in the throes of work, but I take his words to heart. "We'll build in time to meditate for those of us who aren't naturals," I say, just in case the desire or passion to be more Zen is not enough. *(See Strategist as Hustler)*

AFFECTION FOR CHINA

Two Germans, a Persian-German, two Chinese, and a Texan walk into a karaoke bar . . . and we realize we're a walking bad joke. We're led down several dimly lit hallways to the private room they've assigned rOobin and his colleagues. We pass by a number of rooms set up with KTV (as karaoke is called in Asia). Each room has a porthole, so we can peer in and admire the strange décor within. One is Hello Kitty, another is airplane-themed, and our room is reminiscent of Toontown from *Who Framed Roger Rabbit* with animal cartoons making up the mural on one wall.

There are couches built into the back wall, and a ladder leads to more couches above, all of them filled with stuffed animals.

We select Eminem, Bon Jovi, and Bobby McFerrin from a screen in the coffee table and take turns singing along.

I've spent a lot of time with Christian and rOobin, but this outing gives me a chance to get to know rOobin's team better. Tobias went to the same university as rOobin and contacted him looking for work when he decided he wanted to move to China. Stacey and Feifei both grew up in Beijing and discovered advertising through business school. They're all under thirty.

I love hanging out with people from multiple countries. It's what I love most about living in Amsterdam. That I feel most at home among a medley of nationalities makes me think life in China could work for me. I don't think I'd do well as an outsider in a complete monoculture—I'd certainly lose my developing Zen nature in that instance—but I could fall in love with a big city like Beijing. Luckily, this is exactly where any jobs I'd hope to get are located.

It's too loud to have a real conversation in the karaoke room, so I wait until we're at lunch the next day, in a park near the DMG office, to ask rOobin about his perception of expat life in Beijing. We eat at the Stone Boat restaurant, complete with curling roof corners and open-air seating, which sits perched on the edge of a small pond.

"Beijing has become a really cosmopolitan place," he says. "It keeps getting better and better. Now there's good Japanese food, Spanish food, German food . . . if there is such a thing as good German food. It's come a long way in such a short time."

I ask him to reflect on what he sees as the best and worst of Chinese culture. "Compared to German culture, which is a perfection-seeking culture, I now see that getting those last percentage points of perfection doesn't make a huge difference to the quality. Or it makes you too late. I feel there's a certain level of efficiency and effectiveness in not feeling pressure to do things at 100 percent. Maybe that's not the best approach if you're building trains, but with most other things I feel that it's OK not to be a perfectionist. Things can be fixed later. But I also hate it because it can be shortsighted. Sometimes I feel it's obvious that there's a disaster waiting to happen. If people would invest a little more time upfront they would avoid terrible mistakes.

"At DMG, for instance, we would take on too many pitches and too many projects at the same time. That sometimes meant not doing any rehearsals, for example, as we would have done in Europe. The presentation might not feel finished even half an hour before the meeting. Yet you find out that with a certain level of passion it is surprisingly good enough, because there's something at the core that's convincing. And that's something I've learned here. If you go in and fire all the bullets instead of taking aim too long, you end up hitting more targets than you think."

"It's so interesting how living in different countries can change your expectations and expand your views like that. I've been fascinated by some things I've seen here," I say. "Like, I saw a man sleeping on a chain draped between two posts when I was walking over to the office the other morning. He wasn't homeless; he was just taking a nap."

"It's common to see people napping all over the place," he says.

"And while your apartment building is sustainable and modern," I say, "it's been hard not to be repulsed by the air quality at times. For half of my visit here, the air has been fine, but for the other half, it's been hazy and grim. There have been times when I couldn't see across the street. It's like a thick fog."

"It's not a constant thing," he says, "but there are these really terrible days where it's on your radar and you think, *Why the fuck am I doing this, to my children especially?* Then we end up having two weeks of perfect blue skies and brilliant weather, and you start to forget. The best sentence I've ever heard about Beijing: 'Beijing is the worst paradise on Earth.' I think there's so much truth to this. There are a lot of challenges, but there are so many great things here."

As F. Scott Fitzgerald wrote, "The test of a first-rate intelligence is the ability to hold two opposed ideas in the mind at the same time, and still retain the ability to function." I have to wonder, *Am I first-rate enough to handle this place?*

MULTICULTURAL PERSPECTIVE

We head back to rOobin's office. The open-plan space is indistinguishable from most offices around the world, save for a reception area that looks much like the nearby park, even with a little bridge that crosses an in-office koi pond.

"So what's your proudest accomplishment work-wise as you leave DMG?" I ask rOobin.

He looks up and to the left as he thinks for a moment. "For me, it was being part of the Jaguar repositioning. By far."

"Why? What made it such a standout experience?"

"I just feel it was a dying brand that we gave a great identity—one that's completely true to the essence of the brand yet extremely simple to tell somebody and have them understand. If you ask anyone, anywhere in the world, to do word associations with cars, you get a lot of expected answers. BMW, Porsche, and Mercedes are all machines. By contrast, Jaguar, because of the name alone, is an animal."

My eyebrow rises. It's simple but true.

rOobin continues, "As China booms, it's become the top market for many car brands, Jaguar included. So the strategy must work here, and we worked on the position with a global team all together. That meant aligning a group of senior people from different offices around one idea. We landed on the concept of 'Alive.' The people who buy the brand are really living—or they want to see themselves that way, at least.

"I remember one of the earlier ideas was 'Born to Thrill' or 'Natural Born Thriller,' something like that, and one person was fighting very earnestly for it. The idea of being born is fundamental to being alive and does push against the convention of engineering, so it was on strategy, sure. It sounded good in English, but it's a play on words. You can't translate it into German properly; forget about Chinese. And we had to have a global positioning. The thing about 'Alive' is it's a concept, a fundamental human experience that every culture in the world can identify with. It goes beyond language, and that's what makes it so great."

rOobin is trilingual, and now I see the advantage this provides him firsthand. Psychologist Donald Campbell famously studied the impact of knowing more than one culture and concluded that "persons who have been uprooted from traditional cultures, or who have been thoroughly exposed to two or more cultures, seem to have the advantage in the range of hypotheses they are apt to consider, and through this means, in the frequency of innovation." So being a third- or fourth-culture kid like rOobin can impact creativity and problem solving, because you're less rigid in your viewpoints. This type of person knows there are many ways to approach a problem and that there's no one "right" way.

I've also experienced the struggle to articulate an idea across cultures. I worked on a pitch in Holland for a margarine brand, Becel, where the English line used in the UK—"Love their hearts," meaning the margarine was meant to be a demonstration of family love—simply couldn't be communicated in Dutch. The literal translation would mean excluding your own heart. It came off awkward. On the other hand, Emirates' "Hello Tomorrow" was a combination of two fundamental concepts: a greeting of the future. That idea crossed borders.

"The 'Alive' idea is now the blueprint for product design, too," rOobin says. "The ignition button in the car pulsates, like a heartbeat."

I think that's the real test of an idea. If it's expansive and leads to inspiration in the product and other ways of behaving, you know you have something powerful.

BREAKING THROUGH THE EXPAT BUBBLE

It's my last day in Beijing. The rain is light; the day gray, but bright. From my taxi, I see Feifei waiting in front of the temple where we agreed to meet, holding an umbrella. It's not common for a foreigner to be invited to a Chinese person's home, but Feifei, who works on rOobin's team, was willing to buck this convention with a lunch invitation so I could see what her life is like. My interrogation about where she lives might have been perceived as hint dropping. When I get out of the taxi, she greets me, and together we walk through the neighborhood to her apartment building.

We take two flights of stairs. The walls, floors, and stairs are all made of smooth, gray concrete. Her apartment opens directly into the kitchen, where Tientien, her husband, is waiting for us. His name means "wheat wheat," which most Chinese people find funny because here Britney Spears is known as "little wheat wheat." Tientien is watching Chinese *The X Factor* and dicing some vegetables at the kitchen table, which is set snugly between the refrigerator and the wall. After introducing us, Feifei takes me on the quick tour of the other two rooms: their bedroom and the living room.

Feifei has planned to teach me how to make seaweed dumplings for our lunch. They've prepared all of the ingredients already, so the three of us sit at the table, drinking Coke and assemble the dumplings. I love food preparation that takes time and at least a couple of people working together, like shucking fresh peas or rolling stuffed grape leaves.

"This is how you make a perfect dumpling," Feifei says as she sets a round piece of dough down flat and puts a bit of seaweed mixture in the center. Then she wets her fingers with water and lines one half-moon edge. Last, she folds it over and crimps it closed.

Tientien and Feifei move to the cooker and fry the dumplings in one pan and make sautéed bean sprouts in another. Plates of tofu, pork, onions, bread, and sauces are set before me, and then we begin to feast while watching a contestant on *The X Factor* perform.

After lunch, we move to the living room. A very large teddy bear, a gift from Tientien, sits on a large L-shaped couch. Two screens dominate the front wall: a big-screen television and a smaller screen belonging to a computer atop a desk. The patter of rain on glass draws my attention to the far end of the room and a small enclosed porch, where the laundry is set to dry.

Feifei and Tientien are both twenty-six and have been married for less than one year. They've just received their digital wedding photos, and Feifei offers to show them to me. It's common in China to create an album of the happy couple in multiple locations wearing different outfits. We click through the various scenes on her laptop. In one, they are in the Forbidden City, and Feifei is wearing a gorgeous strapless red dress, her hair done in a thirties' style with small waves of hair framing her face. Tientien wears a vest and tie, no jacket. In another, she sits in his lap, arms around his shoulders, as they gaze lovingly into each other's eyes. Her white dress spills across his legs to the floor.

When Tientien goes into the kitchen to make us some tea, Feifei eagerly turns our conversation to her struggle with traditional expectations. She has married before thirty, like she's supposed to, but she wonders about career and children. Her best friend lives in Canada, and so she knows how different life can be in the West. Here, it feels driven mostly by duty. She's supposed to rely on her husband and the family they create for fulfillment, but she wonders if maybe they should go to the US for further degrees.

"What do you think I should do?" she asks.

"I'm still trying to figure these things out myself," I tell her, and then I try to channel the Zen nature that rOobin has imparted to me: "Only you know what's the right path for you," I say. "I really don't believe we can totally screw up our lives, as long as we're learning from each step. I'd never be here if I hadn't failed at love several times. And I'm so grateful to get to meet you and see all these new places."

Because I'm leaving for Shanghai in the morning, Feifei mentions how horrible it is to travel in China. More often than not, public transportation suffers delays, so you can never know if your plane or train will leave on time—which doesn't sound all that different from the rest of the world to me, but she insists it's worse here. Out the window, we can see the rain is really coming down now, and she's worried it may put a crimp in my travel plans to leave Beijing by train because flooding can impact all modes of transport.

They have some shopping to do, and I'm meant to meet rOobin for my last evening in Beijing, so they offer to drive me to his building. In contrast to their humble starter apartment, their car is an impeccable new red Buick. It's a sportier model than they ever built in the US, and I can see how US brands take on different meaning in China. Having this large foreign car is a status symbol, just like almost every other imported American brand here. It looks like China just might give brands like Buick a second chance at life.

Without an umbrella, simply running from the car to rOobin's building has me soaked. Katrin lends me some dry clothes, and we sit around, chatting for hours.

At 11:00 p.m. I realize I'd better get back to the apartment to finish packing up and get to sleep. So rOobin and I go to the lobby of his building and ask for a taxi.

We take a seat and start to chat. The rain has finally slowed after about nine hours, but no taxis are turning up. We sort of lose track of time, and another hour passes. Finally, we decide that perhaps we should walk around outside and head toward a busier intersection to have better luck with finding a cab. Another hour passes, but the Beijing taxi drivers have clearly given up and gone home.

But what's a girl to do when she's stranded without her belongings, and her train is leaving town in the morning? Walking to the apartment isn't a viable option, unless rOobin goes with me and then walks himself home, but that would take two hours or more. His scooter isn't an option either as the roads could be flooded. As the pickle I'm in begins to settle in my mind, a Chinese family in a Honda minivan pulls over and offers me a ride. There are already six in the car—two older women, one older man, and three teen-looking girls. One of the girls is twenty-four and a student at the University of Southern California, so she speaks English.

They give rOobin the impression they know where to take me, and so we say goodbye and begin our journey . . . but after about twenty minutes they pull out a map and we all puzzle over it for a while. I am zero help.

We start driving again, but I'm uncertain I'm ever going to make it until I suddenly realize we're on a road I recognize.

So in the end, I'd managed to get to the apartment via the universal kindness of strangers.

But the drama didn't end there. It turns out, even with the help of a native speaker, I'd managed to buy a train ticket for the wrong date, which the attendant called to my attention as I tried to board the train.

With many flights canceled because of the rain, I was worried about getting to Shanghai as I made my way to the ticket counter to sort out my mistake. The light coming in from the glass roof of the station made me squint as I passed a mixture of Western fast food and Chinese noodle spots to get in the queue. I wanted to be one of those calm travelers who takes what comes at them gracefully—I wanted to channel rOobin's Zen and not care—but my heart beat fast. I hate disappointing people and being late.

I fidgeted and checked my watch while I waited in line. Finally, I got to the front of the line and explained my situation. I couldn't apply my dud ticket toward a new one, but this problem was nothing money couldn't solve. I handed over eight hundred RMB, about eighty euros, and was booked on the next train. I even had time for noodles.

Some things you can't plan, but if you can learn to be Zen, it all works itself out eventually.

STRATEGIST
as hustler

BY rOobin GOLESTAN

I grew up listening to a lot of American rap and hip-hop, and over the last ten or fifteen years I've developed an admiration for Jay-Z in particular. I first thought he was merely exemplifying all that was wrong with hip-hop culture, but if you dig a little deeper you find he's an impressive guy, and there are things about him that you can apply directly to strategy.

There's a lot more to him than the bling bling materialism I first associated with him. He's not formally educated, but as a businessman he's managed to stay culturally relevant, album after album, crafting empire after empire in music, clothes, and now the sports agency business.

Twenty years ago when I started listening to hip-hop, a person like Grandmaster Flash was a grandpa at thirty-two. Jay-Z is forty-three, but he's still one of the most influential people in youth culture. It wasn't even possible to be that close to the pulse of youth at that age in past times. If I think about the sixties, seventies and eighties, culture was always driven by twenty-year-olds and maybe some thirty-year-olds, but definitely not people over forty. Now we're allowed to stay relevant longer. I know this firsthand. I don't feel embarrassed to be DJing at thirty-six. People aren't groaning and saying you're trying too hard to stay young. It's socially acceptable.

There aren't as many things that are just for young people. Boomers love tech and social. Mums are playing lots of games. That's an important shift for brands. This simple fact means that more and more we need to uncover the mind-sets that cross generations rather than recruit some homogenous group of people and psychoanalyze them.

Jay-Z is also street smart. He's observant, and you hear that in his tracks. In *Decoded*, he credits his father for instigating this trait:

My father would take us to Lindy's and we'd get these big-ass steak fries. We would sit in the restaurant looking out the window onto the streets, and play games that exercised our observational skills. Like my pops would make us guess a woman's dress size. There was nothing he missed about a person. He was really good about taking in all the nonverbal clues people give you about their character, how to listen to the matrix of a conversation, to what a person doesn't say.

Who can deny that a strategist needs to be able to pick up on the clues people reveal about themselves, that they may not even realize is the truth and dig deeper than the standard survey answers?

Jay-Z is also a Renaissance man, or what we might call t-shaped. He says, "If people think that I only make music, they're underestimating me. I've been a successful businessman my whole career. I can do more than one thing at one time. I can walk *and* chew gum." It's been talked about a lot, but there's no better thing you can do for your clients than to bring in a lot of inputs. The best ideas are a bricolage of what's on hand that is relevant.

From what I've read about him, Jay-Z is also surprisingly easy for people to work with. Widely different characters, from different backgrounds and eccentric personalities, all get along with him. He gets on with Buffett *and* Bono. He would probably be friends with Frank Sinatra if he were still alive. And isn't that what the best strategists have going for them? The best strategists have an ability to bring lots of different perspectives together by empathizing with every individual on the team and empathizing with real people who might buy our brands. There's no room for divas.

I love how Jay-Z works with language. He doesn't have the most sophisticated lyrics, but they do have double, triple, quadruple meanings. In his words, his music is "dense with multiple meanings. Great rap should have all kinds of unresolved layers that you don't necessarily figure out the first time you listen to it. Instead it plants dissonance in your head. You can enjoy a song that knocks in the club or has witty punch lines the first time you hear it. But great rap retains mystery. It leaves shit rattling around in your head that won't make sense till the fifth or sixth time through. It challenges you." That's what I'm striving for—brand stories that draw people in. Sure, you have to have something for the casual interruption level, but if we can create something interesting, there have to be more layers to create a story, a story that unfolds over time.

Most of all, he's a self-proclaimed hustler. He had a drive to make it to the top and the cunning to get there. It's magical to see a person with a vision and the motivation to make it real. That's what a good strategist does: stays ahead of the game, always proactive, making something from nothing.

care

HARD

ROB CAMPBELL

Wieden+Kennedy | Shanghai

chapter
FOUR

"People don't buy skill in a vacuum. They buy skill plus care."
- Jonathan Fields

It's just a taxi, but this taxi means I made it to Shanghai, and I'm grateful. As I pull away from the train station, which resembles an airport more than any train station I've been to before, dusk begins to settle in, and the last fingers of sun touch the buildings. I'm a time traveler: After four hours propelling across some of China's flat, nondescript expanse listening to a fellow traveler clear his throat every twelve minutes, the gravitational force of this futuristic city is drawing me forward.

The taxi carries me to Shanghai's French Concession. China's architectural modus operandi is to eradicate the buildings of the old dynasty when a new dynasty begins, so, despite five thousand years of history, the highways and office buildings I pass feel more like Dallas than China. There's a Chinese saying that captures their feelings about architecture: "Destroy the old, establish the new."

My host, Rob Campbell, is a bit of a celebrity in adland, not least because he's an outspoken character who's endeared many people through his prolific, provocative blog posts and articles. He's also the head of strategy for the Shanghai office of one of the best ad agencies in the world, Wieden+Kennedy (W+K).

Rob describes himself to everyone as a bald, Queen-loving, Birkenstocks-wearing bloke from Nottingham. I'm hoping to get past this veneer and see if there's more to him than this enumeration of quirks.

In Shanghai, I'm staying in a hotel apartment a block from the agency instead of Rob's home for a couple of reasons: First, I'm terribly allergic to cats, and his cat, Rosie, is far more important to him than some lady he's only met in person once. Second, his wife works from home, designing outrageously artistic cakes, and space is limited. Luckily, his commute from home to work is only a seven-minute walk, and, based on what I know from social media, Rob spends a lot of his time at the office, so hopefully I won't miss too much. I'll simply have to make the most of the time we do spend together.

I exit the taxi on the bustling main road and turn down a *longtang*, one of Shanghai's alleyways, in search of my hotel. There's space enough for pedestrians, bikes, and scooters, but no cars. Fifty paces down the alleyway shields me from the noise, and instead the singing of cicadas fills my ears.

There's no grand entranceway, only an old brass ring hanging from a lion's mouth in the middle of a black lacquer door. I knock three times, and after a moment a man opens the door and peers out. He doesn't speak English but a combination of pantomime and showing my passport earns me an old-fashioned brass key.

The man leads me up two flights of black shellacked stairs that hug the walls and lead to various landings. The hotel is named Kevin's Old House, but by "old" they certainly don't mean five thousand years. If I had to guess, I'd say one hundred years isn't far off, though I can't think of any historical figures named Kevin, be they from five thousand years ago or one hundred.

My room is quite large, with a huge four-poster bed, armoire, baroque style sofa, heavy velvet curtains, and dark wood floors. It feels Shanghai-chic to me. The antique lamps, desk, and claw-foot bathtub seem fit for a visiting empress.

I head back out to find a spot for dinner. The neighborhood is full of character with low two-story buildings and tree-lined streets. I stroll past boutiques, galleries, and unassuming micro-restaurants. A makeshift kitchen spills out onto the sidewalk. Inside, an older man wearing an apron shovels noodles into a bowl. His face is partially obscured by the rising steam from the wok. Though his concoction smells good, I decide I'd rather sit at a table than grab a quick side-of-the-road fill-up, so I keep walking.

The street lamps begin to come on, and I find a quintessential Chinese restaurant. All the cues are there: red walls, gold accents, and lion statues. I'm a bit impatient for the next day as I take a table alone and choose some dumplings and sautéed greens. Chinese families and expats fill the tables around me.

In the morning, I walk one block to the appointed address, but I'm not exactly certain of which door to enter. I see a guy wearing a T-shirt, shorts and black-rimmed glasses walking through an open gate, and my ad-dar is triggered. I follow him into an elevator and ask if he knows Rob. Luckily he does, and I'm delivered to Rob's desk moments later.

"Bloody hell, you're here!" Rob says, his eyes sparkling behind his glasses. He's wearing an AC/DC T-shirt, loose jeans, and, of course, Birkenstocks.

OUR TRUSTING CONNECTION

Rob and I first came to know each other through the survey. I'd asked respondents to name companies they thought had the best strategy departments, and a place I hadn't heard of, Sunshine, came up in the results. I gave it an honorable mention in the report, saying I'd like to learn more, and Rob, who cofounded the company, promptly wrote to alleviate me of my ignorance. Later, when he joined W+K Shanghai, he started coming to Amsterdam occasionally, and so we finally had the chance to meet for coffee. Our first meeting turned out to be a catalyst for a strange series of events.

It started out completely normal. I was riding my bike along a canal, heading toward our meet-up spot, when I noticed a man wearing Birkenstocks . . . in November. Must be Rob. I pulled over, and we began a nonstop gabathon. When we sat down for coffee, he asked about my new job at StrawberryFrog, and I told him of a strange experience where a new hire I made never arrived on the day he was meant to start. The new hire—let's call him "Max"—texted me in the middle of the night on his start date to say his sister had been in a terrible car accident and he wouldn't be able to fly over from London as planned. Weeks went by, and I received only a couple of messages from him. He told me he'd have to donate part of his liver for her survival, and that his recovery would take six weeks or more. He'd type that he still wanted the job but then wouldn't return my calls and actually speak with me. After several weeks of this, and despite his good references and his insistence he was eager to work with us, my colleagues and I decided to write him off. We just didn't know what to think.

That is, until I met with Rob. After I told him the story, he revealed that he knew Max too, and that he'd heard this story almost word for word before. Only it had happened to someone else in Australia.

After our coffee, Rob put me in touch with the people Max had worked with in Australia and I discovered a similar scenario had happened there and also in the US.

This set me off on a weeklong investigation. I barely slept. Friends of mine around the world helped me investigate and piece together a picture of Max as a con man rather than the promising young strategist I thought I'd hired. "Con man" is a weird word to use, but there isn't anything more apt; Max didn't get much out of the scam other than the ego boost of a job offer. Yet, we discovered, he'd played out this "terrible accident" drama five times.

Convinced he would never stop of his own volition, I decided to reveal Max's deception on my blog to stop this sort of scenario from happening yet again.

This incident taught me several things, namely that there is a difference between being gullible and being trusting. While I thought I was the former, through a few e-mails Rob helped me see myself as the latter.

"If you assume everyone is out to get you," he wrote, "you're less likely to be deceived. But you're also less likely to meet wonderful people you wouldn't have met normally, and that would be a shame."

I'm the sort of person who goes on blind dates and finds workout partners by placing ads on Craigslist. Psychologists call behaviors such as these "risky social interactions."

Rob does these things, too. For example, he and a few other strategists take turns offering strategic assignments on their blogs and judging the responses to help young people get more experience in the field. He's met every single person I've sent his way for coffees, even though he and I have only ever met in person once. And, duh, he's let that "only met once" gal come and stalk him at his job.

What Rob helped me understand is that we're not fools. We're trusting.

And there's a difference.

CULTIVATING INFORMANTS

Like the other W+K offices I've visited in Portland and Amsterdam, the interior of the Shanghai location is architecturally stunning. It's an open-plan space that combines concrete, metal, glass, and graffiti artwork. To me, these details reveal a company run by creative people. At the other end of the spectrum are the large global conglomerates run by finance people. Correlation does not equal causation, but I believe, in this case, space influences output.

Rob takes up two tables in the middle of an open pool of desks: one table for his computer and papers, and the other for a selection of guitars, harkening back to his first career as a session guitarist for eighties' pop stars. Swapping music for advertising took him to work in Australia, London, the US, Singapore, and Hong Kong before landing in Shanghai. He has me drop my things at a desk just behind his and leads me into a conference room.

"How are things going so far with your trips?" Rob asks as we both take a seat. He leans back and smiles, radiating warmth.

"Really well," I say. "I'm certainly learning things, but it's still not clear how this will all become a book. I'm taking lots of notes."

"What are you hoping to get out of this trip?" he asks. "Not just here, but the whole journey?"

I think for a minute. I probably want too much from this project. I'd be most happy with a clear direction to take my career next after all these trips.

"I'm hoping that one of these visits will lead to a job," I say. "Maybe not necessarily on one of your teams, but perhaps through the people I meet. I want to have that same drive I felt when I left the US and moved to Amsterdam. That move was so right for me that it felt like the only sane thing I could do at the time.

"Maybe it's too soon to tell, but I don't get the sense that there are so many jobs in China. rOobin told me there are probably less than sixty or eighty strategists in Beijing, so I'm guessing that means there are around one hundred in Shanghai?"

"That's probably generous," Rob replies.

"When I started, I really thought I'd end up in Asia. I suppose I'm adjusting my expectations as I go along. Just picking up ideas and books and things from the people I'm meeting. And seeing that I can jump in and have an impact in a short period of time is building my confidence. I did a week of freelance in Tokyo with Uniqlo before I came over to China, and they were almost in awe of the way I saw the problem. Or they were just being polite." I smile. "It was hard to tell."

"I think this trip is a reboot for you. I don't think anyone feels confident all the time, but you've got some pretty big touchstones to turn to, like the survey. When that came out, I just thought it was genius. I thought, why has no one thought of this before? I'm sure people had thought about doing it, but you fucking did it. And that's the difference. And that's why you doing this project is the difference. People talk about writing a book, but if you say it, you have to do it. I think that's wonderful."

His compliment washes over me. It's intensely flattering to hear this out loud. Sure, people have thanked me and told me that the survey was well done and that this book idea is smart, but given that Rob knows the background of this project and that I don't always feel confident, his praise really means a lot.

"In a perfect world," Rob says, "you'd be able to speak Mandarin fluently, and I'd send you out on a brand assignment. But you don't, so I thought I'd give you an assignment that isn't dependent on language. I want you to go out and interview Westerners living here about what it means to live in China as an outsider. What's changed while they've been here? What's most notably different from where they come from?

"I want you to learn for yourself what it would be like to live here. Most expats go home having learnt 10 percent of the language, if that. They've never been in the home of a Chinese person. They go to the Great Wall and the Terra Cotta soldiers, but they never travel to a two-thousand-year-old village. If you do come over here, I expect you'd dig into it more deeply, but this is a start to help you see a possible future. And it could help me on a few things I'm working on, too."

"Thanks, Rob. This sounds amazing," I say, eager to see what I will find. "I want to try out your methods as much as I can." I think back to when I first met Rob and he told me about a unique way of working he'd developed. To get to fresh ideas no one had thought before, he'd interview "informants" such as priests, prostitutes, or professors. "Can you tell me more about working with informants?" I ask him. "Maybe I can fold that into my approach."

"Sure, sure. Well, I always look for interesting people with an undeniable credibility. A prostitute makes assumptions of a man based on the car he drives, for example, and I think that a car brand ought to know what it is. Not for shock value, but for purpose. I'm always looking for a point of view others might not have realized. Now, it doesn't always work. Once, we were working on a beauty brand, and I wondered if women with bad acne have different haircuts. I asked Sue, one of my team, to go talk to hairdressers. Turns out they don't."

I loved this idea of Rob's to cultivate informants from the moment I heard it. It makes this job feel more like film noir or hard-hitting investigative journalism. But I've never had the, ahem, *cojones* to talk to a prostitute. What if I were to waste a lot of time chasing down input but nothing comes of it? Thought leaders in a category are one thing, but interviewing outsiders who are not obviously relevant could put a dent in my own credibility. However, I'm excited to have the leeway to explore.

"I'm shameless," Rob says. "If I see a documentary with someone interesting, I'll write to that person and invite them for a coffee—even if it means flying to another country. I have the means to feed my obsession with interesting people, so I collect them. You never know when their insight might prove useful."

In their book *The Start-up of You*, Reid Hoffman and Ben Casnocha seem to agree with Rob and advise everyone to set up an "interesting people fund" to dedicate money to meeting interesting people. If new ways of approaching a problem are valuable, it makes sense that you would invest in amassing such a network. Sadly, I can't imagine a company supporting such a speculative initiative.

I suppose I've dabbled in this arena in my day-to-day work, too. When I was working on the launch for Gucci Guilty, which is a fragrance based on the idea of transgression and a dark aesthetic, I asked my then-boyfriend to help me think about the strategy. Because of his experience making dark, electronic music and photographing fetish parties in Amsterdam in his spare time, I'd met a lot of his friends in this world; half were very ordinary people who simply like to dress up occasionally, and the other half chose this aesthetic as a defining characteristic of their identity. Knowing these people and seeing the events they go to helped me to describe the type of transformational experience we were trying to achieve with a digital experience for Gucci. I would never have approached the assignment this way if I hadn't met this group of people.

But Rob takes this further and proves you can spot people who perhaps seem unapproachable—for example, prostitutes—and succeed in speaking with them if you are respectful. (See *Informants for Business*)

Given my assignment, I try to think about interesting ways to approach expats in Shanghai. I look for networking events on LinkedIn. I message a few of the more vocal expats on Twitter. I spend some time on an expat dating site and contact a few of the less creepy options. Luckily, a fellow Texan quickly responds, and I have a lunch date set up for the next day. Then an e-mail arrives in my inbox. . . .

It's from a young strategy upstart, Erika Brenner, a Brazilian transplant to China who's spent the last two years learning Mandarin and who's trying to break into the work scene here. She'd noticed me suddenly joining some Shanghai-based LinkedIn groups and asked if I was coming to town. I send her a reply to say I'm already in town. We decide to meet for dumplings on Wednesday night. In just a couple of hours, I've found my own informants. Is it really this easy?

GETTING UNDER CHINA'S SKIN

Later that afternoon, Rob pulls Tom, one of his strategists, and me into a conference room to take me through another project. W+K is pitching a Chinese brand of a common, everyday product. I'll keep the brand and the product a mystery for confidentiality's sake, but the details really aren't important. What *is* important? The public perception of a product that's "made in China." Prejudices against Chinese-made products persist within the country too: Many locals prefer imported goods to those locally made. The global perception of goods made here means that hardly any local brands have managed to make the crossover to dominate international markets the way Western brands have penetrated Chinese society.

Ironically, some of the most admired brands in the world make their products here, but that has not enabled people to like, trust, or respect brands that originate in China. This mystery brand is aiming to change these perceptions. They want to do something great for China. They want to create the first world-class, modern Chinese brand.

"This brand is fundamentally about empowering Chinese people," Rob explains. "They're fighting for integrity and honor with a Chinese brand so that the Chinese people can feel integrity and honor."

Though home to massive businesses like Alibaba (an online market), Xiaomi (a smartphone producer), and WeChat (a messaging app), these businesses aren't originals, but they do improve upon existing ideas through efficiency and scale. Chinese ingenuity looks different than what we might expect in the West. And while ancient China invented the compass, gunpowder, paper, and moveable type, modern China is better known for the fastest rise from poverty in human history by making simple businesses highly profitable. While this is beginning to change, in this context an innovative company might make quite the meaningful mark.

Because it's being built from scratch, this brand is poised to scrap the category conventions and start fresh. Rob asks Tom and me to brainstorm other brands that have transformed staid categories. What attributes do Saturn cars, Burberry, and Method cleaning supplies share?

"When I think of these sort of upstart brands," Tom says, "they all seem to be hungrier than the incumbents in their categories. A lot of times they have a visionary leader, too."

"They almost always speak directly to a cultural tension," I add. "Saturn took on the convention of haggling over the price, and Method challenged the lack of style and beauty among cleaning products. What do you think the tension is here?"

"Lack of status," Rob says. "Status is unbelievably important in China. There's a social prejudice against products made in China, especially a product with a comparably low price. Its perceived status will be low. What people say and do here is almost always the opposite. They'd rather cry in a BMW than be happy on a bicycle."

Because this product isn't exceptionally expensive, it won't immediately convey status like luxury brands in the category convey.

"We'll need to bring the story of what China is doing to reinvent [this category] in a way that will inspire a nation," Rob says.

This seems to be the underlying need for most of the brands W+K work with in China. For example, the London Olympics are happening during my visit, and P&G (a W+K client) launched the global "Proud Sponsor of Moms" campaign. In it, you see mothers from all around the world doing all the things moms do to take care of everything behind the scenes and support their young athletes.

Late on Thursday evening at the office, Rob shows me the campaign on his laptop and teaches me about the different sacrifices Chinese mothers make compared to Western mothers. In China, promising athletic children are often sent away from their families to develop their abilities at government-sponsored facilities, which changes the context of being the mother of an athlete.

"That's why I get annoyed at terms like 'global human truths,'" he tells me, "because people think that means everyone does the same thing, but it's rubbish.

Sure, mums all around the world love their kids, but how a mum demonstrates or expresses that in Wuhan, China, will be very different to how a mum would in Seattle, USA. The emotions may be the same, but the context is entirely different."

Rob seems doggedly driven to uncover these sorts of differences, which seem to be the secret to crafting meaningful stories for brands. I'm impressed by the fascination factor of this new culture, but more so by Rob's determination, as an outsider, to really understand the living algorithm of Chinese culture.

HUSBAND-HUNTING IN SHANGHAI

It's a warm summer Saturday, and Erika, my Brazilian expat informant, is standing in as a surrogate mother for me. Which is weird, not least because she's ten years younger than me. We've chosen a spot in the shade, and it doesn't take long for several curious bystanders to start reading my ad. They engage Erika in doubtful banter about the likelihood of my finding a match today.

We've come to this corner of People's Park for the Marriage Market, where parents put out simple, single-sheet ads on the ground describing their unmarried children for other parents to peruse.

After two years of applying herself to learning Mandarin, Erika has created an ad for me on a standard sheet of paper:

AMERICAN WOMAN LOOKING FOR A BOYFRIEND

NAME: Heather
COUNTRY: United States of America
HEIGHT: 1.82m

JOB: Boss of advertising company (Consultant)

REQUIREMENTS: 1.90m or above, between 30 and 40 years old, has a good job, able to speak English (important), likes to travel, willing to live abroad.

Our height request makes every parent who reads my ad laugh. When they express disbelief that we'll find anyone who meets this requirement, we remind them of Yao Ming, the seven-foot, six-inch Shanghai-born former NBA player. Surely there are a few less famous Chinese men who are taller than me? All of the parents carry small photo albums full of pictures of their child, but the sons on offer are all a head shorter than me and don't speak English.

Far from being offended, as we worried they might be, the parents who talk with us mainly laugh at the good joke we've provided among the serious business of matchmaking going on around us. Nevertheless, it's clear that expats are expected to date other expats, not their sons.

We meet a professor, Dr. Jiang, a Chinese gentleman who lives in California but is visiting Shanghai. He's come to the park to look for a wife for his son.

"What do you think about this practice of a market to match up sons and daughters like this?" I ask him.

"I think it's a very practical way to start the dating process," he tells me. "It's a microcosm of society here in the dating corner."

"And what do you think my chances of finding a man here are?"

He smiles, his face ruddy and shiny from the heat. "On the one hand, you're a very attractive girl, and a Caucasian, which is kind of high on the market in terms of value, OK? On the other hand, you're a really tall girl, which is not normal here. And you want someone with the right job and the right open-minded personality. It will be like hitting the lottery to find a dating partner here."

I laugh. "Thanks for sugarcoating it, Dr. Jiang!"

Erika and I decide to cut our losses and go out for hot pot. Who needs a husband when you can learn about a new culture through the eyes of your informant instead?

NOT EVIL, DEVIOUS

Like many agencies, the W+K kitchen has snacks on hand to keep the collective blood sugar up. But instead of cereal, W+K Shanghai offers dumplings and noodles first thing in the morning. Each day I try coming in a little bit earlier, grab a few dumplings, and walk up the central staircase to the top floor. I always find Rob already at his desk.

It's in these early hours before work begins or in the evenings when the staff thins out that he has more time to chat about his ways of working. I settle in, and Rob picks up our conversation from the night before as though eight hours had not passed.

"Good morning, lovely," Rob says.

"Good morning, boss," I say. "What are you working on?"

"I was writing a blog post before everyone gets in. You know you mentioned seeing yourself as a muse and it got me thinking. . . . For me, I see myself at the creative end of business rather than at the business end of creativity. They may sound similar, but the difference is huge. Being at the creative end of business means you want to seek out your clients' bigger business problems, not just their marketing and communication needs. It means you want to use creativity in broader and more interesting ways. It means you want to develop solutions that are amplified through communication rather than the solution always being communication. Of course, for this to happen, you need clients to let you at their bigger challenges—but in my experience, that can only happen if you start being interested in what they need, not what you want them to need."

One of the methods Rob has developed to generate ideas at the creative end of business he calls "devious strategy." He described it on his blog as "the development of an idea that gives your audience something they specifically want, but delivered in a way that also fulfills your own personal—and totally different—set of goals and agenda." (See *Devious Strategy*)

Most of the examples Rob gives me of the devious strategies he's tried with clients he asks me not to share, so I press him for publicly available instances of devious strategy in action.

"I did hear about something I thought was brilliant," Rob tells me. "When Daniel Radcliffe [aka Harry Potter] was in New York for several months acting in a play, he found himself pestered by the paparazzi. However, he didn't try to persuade them to leave him alone. Instead, he decided to let the paparazzi take pictures if they wanted, but he'd wear the exact same clothes every day. For tabloid readers, it would look like one endless day. So of course, the paparazzi got bored and left him alone."

"I see what you mean," I say. "It's more of a 'rising tide lifts all boats' way of looking at the world." I vow to be more devious henceforth.

IF I WERE TO MOVE TO CHINA

After nearly two weeks of stalking expats in malls, cafés, and over the Internet, I assembled what I'd learned to share with Rob. We sit at the conference room table, and I share my informant interactions and list of best quotes.

"You went on a date to meet an expat?" he asks, disbelieving.

"Well, he's Texan, too, but there was no love connection," I reply. "I suspect we'll stay friends though. He's a singer/songwriter. Perhaps a future informant for another project?"

I explain that, in addition to the typical vox pop interruptus method, I also invited myself to Erika's mother's book club to interact with a slew of Brazilian transplants. "I know it's a small sample, but the people I was able to reach through an interest in them—the ladies' book club, going on a date, setting up an ad at the marriage market—were way more insightful than those I accosted at cafés."

"Yes! Informants in action," he says. "Now what did you learn?"

I tell him about the expat taxonomy that emerged, which consisted of two main groups: those who had a burning desire, or at least an itching curiosity, to come to China, and those who felt that they were escaping economic malaise or violence in their home country. The first group is like da Gama or Pizarro exploring uncharted territories and meeting alien cultures—minus the imperialist tendencies. The second group reminds me of the pilgrims—minus the buckled shoes.

There are the practical reasons to live here. You can outsource all of your household work easily, which means you can work and still have a life. You can have a child and still meet friends out for dinner. Women especially find Shanghai more livable than the West.

And there are the cultural reasons to live here. Chinese culture is full of contradictions. Old and new. Loud and quiet. And there's a stereotype that Chinese people aren't creative because they learn by rote, but you see so much evidence to the contrary. People have businesses where employees play World of Warcraft to sell hard-earned virtual weapons. The government instituted a scratch-off lottery on sales receipts to encourage citizens to ask for them when they buy anything, from a meal to a dress, in order to squash tax fraud. When it comes to making money, the Chinese can get incredibly creative.

"Personally, what I love about it here is that it forces you to reexamine things you've taken for granted," Rob says. "I like to be forced to look at things in a new light. I like positive conflict. Like coming to China in the first place. Or having you here. I always wanted to be able to look back at the end of my life and be able to say, 'You cheeky little bugger.' I'm certain my time in China is helping in that respect."

CHARISMA AS BUSINESS TOOL

Over and above his subversive workaholic personality, Rob is charismatic. That's simple to say, but when you unpack his unique charisma recipe, there are many elements to it. He's self-deprecating. He's funny. He really listens. He knows how to share his way of thinking with confidence.

There's a prevailing belief that you're either born charismatic or you're not, but Olivia Fox Cabane counters this notion in her book *The Charisma Myth*. "Charisma is a result of a set of behaviors. Not an innate or natural quality," she says. As a socially inept teen, she decided to figure out "this human thing" and learned to gradually gain charisma herself. She also points to Steve Jobs, who, like her, learned to conquer his nerdy, awkward, nervous persona and emerge as a charismatic person.

In the book, she breaks down charismatic behaviors into three categories: presence, power, and warmth. I can see evidence of all three in Rob. He does that Bill Clinton thing of giving whoever he's talking to his entire attention.

Cabane says men are often uncomfortable with warmth, but this is where I think Rob is especially different. From sharing his love of his mum, to the pain of losing his father, Rob is able to be vulnerable. He also has no trouble expressing his genuine interest in others.

On my last day, Rob takes me for an Italian lunch—in Shanghai. We munch on focaccia in a cozy café with grapevines hand-painted on the walls.

"Do you think you're charismatic?" I ask. "Do you do the Bill Clinton thing where people feel they are the only person in the room on purpose?"

"That's a hard question, because you're essentially asking if I'm consciously taking an interest in someone. The answer is yes and no. Yes because I was brought up by my parents to always 'care about what others care about.' My dad was very charismatic and would never hesitate to talk with people. And my mum was incredibly empathetic and would almost feel what others were saying rather than just listen. But it's also no, because it's not done in an attempt to manipulate people. I can honestly say I'm not actively looking for the good in people, and I certainly wouldn't pretend to like or agree with people I don't respect or actually agree with. Many of my clients and colleagues would testify to this." He laughs. "But when I meet individuals who are genuine in their intent and passionate about their beliefs and views, I love to listen and learn so I can get a better understanding of where they're coming from."

Our meals arrive, and we both tuck in. I'm beginning to realize that what makes Rob special is just how much he cares.

"There have also been times in my career where I've had to tell someone, 'Don't mistake my humor for not being professional or obsessed with doing the best,'" he says. "Maybe that's because people don't think you can or should be openly enthusiastic and conduct business at the same time, but I passionately believe charisma and personality have commercial value. Business schools would be smart to spend some time on those sorts of behaviors and not just the quantifiable aspects of management and decision making."

In my opinion, Rob is excellent at communicating effectively and at making strong interpersonal connections. He's not just a smiling face. He's smart without taking on the persona of intellectual bully that some strategists assume. And he cares hard. What I mean by that is that he's in it, fully committed to doing his best and getting the best out of others without sacrificing the joy. He's managed to preserve his soul while embracing the corporate world.

THE SENSITIVE OUTLAW

After two weeks, I've only briefly shaken hands with Jill and have not yet stepped foot into their flat.

"Do you think I could see your house?" I ask Rob on our last day.

"Of course," he says. "The time has really flown by, hasn't it?" He cheerily leads me three blocks east of the office to an eight-story apartment building.

The apartment is very tidy, with a modern kitchen immediately in view upon entering. The dining and living areas are open, and floating shelves line the walls with an array of books, clocks, and robot pets. The walls are covered in an eclectic mix of contemporary original artworks and pieces from IKEA. Like his office, there are more guitars in stands, perfectly kerned, against the wall. Hundreds of DVDs are stacked near the television.

Jill is out with a friend, so the apartment is oddly quiet compared to this boisterous man I've gotten to know over these two weeks.

"And this is our room," Rob says as he walks into the last room. He even opens his closet to reveal meticulously stacked piles of denim and T-shirts and rows of neatly placed Birkenstocks. "I can't show you Jill's closet," he chuckles.

To me, it's odd that he's willing to show me his closet at all. Jason, Simon, and rOobin certainly didn't include their closets on the tours of their homes.

"You seem so open with your life," I say. "You're always posting your latest gadget or Jill's cakes or pictures of Rosie on Facebook. But—and I don't mean to sound accusatory—I did have to invite myself over to see it in person."

"Well, I give a huge amount of myself to work, so I purposefully create a separation of work and home," he tells me. "I want to make sure the time I spend at home is quality time."

While I feel like I've momentarily upset this balance, I'm grateful not just for this tour but for the full two-week intrusion into Rob's life. I know he won't hold it against me. He's too good-hearted. And it shows he cares so much about his work that he was willing to share with me. That care and extra effort is what I feel makes Rob an extraordinary strategist. If I want to be one as well, I can never let up in my pursuit of excellence.

INFORMANTS
for business

BY ROB CAMPBELL

I honestly can't remember when I first got the idea for informants, but I know where it stems from. When I was a kid, my house was full of interesting people. My dad was a wonderful man, and he wanted me to experience all kinds of people. So if he met a homeless person, for example, he would offer him a bath, a hot meal, and a bed for the night, but they had to agree to talk to his son. I fell in love with people's stories. I genuinely believe everyone has a story. It's just part of who I am.

Cut to working in this business. If there's one thing I'm good at, it's knowing what I'm bad at. And I'm not going to be one of those people who tries to bullshit my way and pretend I know something if I don't. Clients generally know a lot about their own business. If you try to fake it, they will know. And worse, they may not tell you to your face. You go away thinking, "I'm cool" only to find out later that you're shit.

For me, being a good partner has always been about bringing in fresh thinking. One way I do that is by seeking the opinions of people I find interesting, in any field of life who have relevant knowledge, but knowledge that perhaps has never been considered previously.

I think the first time I ever sought out an informant was for a car radio company. They made one of the first stylish, well-designed sound systems and this client was looking to us to help them launch it. The sound was great, but it also looked shit-hot. I'd seen a program about a young kid who stole cars and I thought he might have a unique perspective on this radio, so I tracked him down through friends of friends. I got hold of him and managed to get to talk to him.

He had an amazing insight. He said if we promoted this thing the way the client wanted to, as a fashion piece, he'd be hired to steal it. And if enough of them were stolen, no one would want to buy them anymore.

I brought him to the meeting, and I remember feeling empowered. No clients are ever going to give me the right to say something about their brand just because I work in advertising. But someone who has undeniable credibility? They will listen. And being the person who brought in someone with undeniable credibility? That, they'll remember.

To do this, I collect interesting people. I was once on a plane from Hong Kong to the Philippines and the strangest thing happened. It was completely empty, but I was next to this other guy. He heard me talking and must have noticed my accent. Turns out we we're both from Nottingham and both Forest fans. We get to talking, and he reveals he's the chief of police for the fraud department. I started to wonder how much stuff he knows that he doesn't know he knows. Not anything private, just what he's picked up along the way. I asked him which brands criminals copied the most. At the time, it was Miu Miu.

Now, criminals don't do anything that's not financially motivated. There are loads of popular fashion brands, but isn't it fascinating to know that at that moment in time, Miu Miu was being copied the most? It's like getting to peek at their sales figures for the next quarter. I realized I now knew something as an outsider that only an insider would know.

I've talked to priests and prostitutes. Yes, prostitutes. If you're a bloke of a certain age and you sit in a hotel bar, you're going to be approached. Just by being honest and offering to buy them drinks, women have given me all manner of incredible insight into behavior that has unexpected relevance.

I struggle with this industry because it's supposed to represent the masses, the human experience, but it's forgotten how to talk to human beings and, more often than not, it acts robotic. Cultivating informants proves that I care. We're so desperate to pretend that we know everything. We don't know everything. I think we should know what society thinks and feels better than anyone else. The only way to get there is by talking to people.

I base what I do on hint and hunch. I never go in saying, "This is the right answer." What I say is, "This suggests that . . . and these are some hypotheses." Time after time, it has given me an early start. And when I'm working with clients, I have this trove of anecdotes that can come from anywhere to help demonstrate a point.

I'm a bald-headed English bloke in China. How the fuck do I know anything? But when I ask people questions, they give me answers.

BY ROB CAMPBELL

What a lovely provocative title, especially as the reality is it's simply about "being clever."

The expression was born from my study of the Chinese government—a group who, in my opinion, are some of the greatest strategists that have ever lived. I am in awe at how they manage their country.

Not just that they found a way to balance their communist ideals while encouraging and exploiting capitalist attitudes and behavior (both internally and externally), but they've managed to do it in a way that lets people embrace the new opportunities available to them while keeping the country relatively stable and committed to the current power structure.

Sure, you could argue that this has been achieved through a mix of fear and propaganda—and obviously there's more than an element of truth in that—but the fact is, they've achieved this by always being in control of the outcome.

Case in point: The Internet.

The government probably wished they never had to give their people access to it.

Sure, they understood there were massive commercial benefits to digital. The government has embraced and exploited that—hence brands like Twitter and Facebook have been kicked out so the revenue of the local equivalent stays in China. However, life would have been much easier if they had been able to keep it away from the masses.

Of course they couldn't—and didn't—and one of the reasons was they didn't want to be negatively labeled as an oppressive regime by foreign governments. These are organizations they want to keep relatively happy so investments keep rolling in.

So they answered their conundrum by simply giving the masses slow Internet. This ensured they could censor, manage, and observe what's going on while still being able to say they have let a billion people have access to the World Wide Web.

It's bloody genius.

I think cause marketing can also be "devious." I once proposed to Virgin that they stop all advertising and give the money to the National Health Service (NHS). They didn't do it, but my premise was the positive impact it could have would outweigh both the "exploitative" screams we would encounter as well as the advertising noise we had to fight each and every day.

The problem I have with a lot of people regarding cause marketing is they seem to think making money is a bad thing and the only way a company can show its good intentions is to do things for free. I think this is bullshit.

Money makes the world go round. The more you have, the more—potentially—you can fix, influence, and help. So for me, my view is to directly help our clients make more money but in ways that naturally aids causes. There is absolutely nothing wrong with making oodles of cash; it's how you do it and what you do with it once you've got it that's key.

The sooner we realize that the way to get corporations to help society is—ironically—to help the corporation make money, the sooner we will develop ideas that have real traction and impact.

Of course, it's not easy developing concepts that naturally aid communities while helping the clients profitability (à la "Tesco Computers for Schools"), but if we're as smart as we think we are, we should be able to do it.

stay on the FRINGE

PHIL ADAMS

Blonde Digital | Edinburgh

chapter FIVE

**"Don't be too timid and squeamish about your actions.
All life is an experiment."**

– Ralph Waldo Emerson

When I blogged my intention to do this project, Phil Adams was first to comment: "If you fancy a wee stint in Edinburgh—maybe during the Festival—let me know. It's not Rio de Janeiro, but . . . "

I didn't know Phil. We hadn't exchanged any e-mails, blog comments, or Twitter replies before. However, since by chance we were both going to London on business at the same time, we decided to meet for lunch in Soho. Phil, forty-something with salt-and-pepper hair, works as the head of strategy for Blonde Digital, a digital agency in Scotland. Blonde is known for its clever work for IRN-BRU (a native Scottish fizzy drink) as well as the UK's Royal Mail, and I'm especially interested to expand on my experience at Tribal and spend more time in a digital agency. Given the rapid changes happening in marketing due to what new technology is making possible, I'd like to see as many ways of working in this space as possible.

Our meeting, which Phil now describes as his "interview," gave us both a chance to turn avatar into person. And it gave me the chance to see that Phil had a lot to offer as a coach. We left the meeting with a plan in place for me to visit a few months later in August, when the Fringe Festival was taking place.

DAUGHTER NUMBER FIVE

There's something a little awkward about getting picked up at the airport by someone you don't really know. The alternative—arriving at their place of work or even their home—means a tour of the space, which creates instant conversation. Also, other people (especially children) distract and ease the transition from acquaintance to friend. But it wasn't going to play out that way this time. Nope. Phil had forced his kindness on me and refused to let me take a taxi to his home, so it would be just me and Phil at the airport.

He spots me leaving the secure section of the airport, smiles shyly, and gives a little wave.

The flight from Amsterdam to Edinburgh was only an hour and a half. Despite the quick trip, I feel hesitant, as if I'm a foreign exchange student arriving to meet my host family. As we exit the airport, I find it's surprisingly cold for August. Phil begins to load my luggage into the back of an oversized SUV.

"Right." English pause. "Just two weeks?" he asks, mostly kidding as he heaves my larger case into the car.

"Well, I won't need to do any laundry," I say, smiling. "Surely you know that women don't always pack as light as men?"

If any man were to know the secrets of my gender, it would be Phil Adams. He's been outnumbered by the fairer sex for a very long time. With four daughters, he trumps all previous hosts with the size of his brood.

As we set off, driving north, Phil warns me what I'm in for while living with his family. "It certainly won't be dull," he tells me.

We drive away from Edinburgh, across an inlet of the North Sea, and, just as the clear, bright day is ending, we pass over the Forth Road Bridge into the county of Fife. The rolling farmland is punctuated by roundabouts, and in the distance the Pentland Hills frame an ASDA supermarket.

We turn off the main road onto a bumpier private road that cuts through paddocks dotted with horses and bales of hay. The road ahead inclines upward and weaves into the tree line before becoming completely hidden from the main road. Now I understand why Phil insisted on collecting me at the airport: No taxi would be able to find this place.

We emerge from the trees, and Phil parks between the house, which is on the right side of the drive, and the large shed on the other. The back door opens, and two dogs sprint out to sniff and attempt to knock me over as I get out of the car. The air is crisp and smells incredibly clean.

Phil moan-shouts, "Aw, Ky, Harvey, get down!"

The dogs back off, and a girl emerges from the house and comes to investigate the new arrival. Phil introduces me to his youngest, eight-year-old Madeleine, and then leads us inside.

We walk through a three-season room with lots of windows and straight into the kitchen, where there's a long oak table and an antique stove radiating warmth.

Just off the kitchen is the piano room, which the family has sacrificed for me. A pop-up queen-size bed takes up most of the center of the room. The French doors on the other end look out to their back garden, and the view sweeps downward over the horse paddocks, which we'd driven across on our way to the house. In the distance is the sea.

The sounds of more people spill from the kitchen, and we return to greet the rest of the family, who have just arrived back from a shopping trip.

Rachel, Phil's wife, puts down the groceries. "Heather, we're so pleased to have you here!" Her eyes sparkle and she rounds up the other girls to meet me: Molly, fifteen, is pretty and shy like her dad. Lois, thirteen, is as tall as Molly and instantly polite. Penny, twelve, is the only daughter with brown hair, and she's clearly the mischievous one because she's already taunting Madeleine about having to take a bath before dinner.

Rachel runs both hands through her short, coppery blonde hair and orders the group into action. At her command, the bath and dinner are under way. The two cats scurry out, lest they be given a chore, too. Phil pulls out some wine, and we all chat between the chopping and sautéing.

"Mum! Madeleine won't let me comb her hair!" Penny announces as she chases Madeleine back into the kitchen after the bath. Madeleine is sobbing, clearly tortured by Penny and her own tangled locks.

"I know something about long hair," I say, and offer to give it a go and try to make myself useful.

Madeleine agrees, hands me her comb, and sits at the kitchen table.

I stand behind her and try to slowly work all the knots out of her hair while Phil, devoted family historian, snaps a picture of us—Madeleine in mid-pout. He's posting it on Instagram as the family sits down to dinner.

BLONDE WITH A BRAIN

Phil's commute the next morning has us backtrack by car down the hill, across the paddocks and over to the commuter rail station. We park and catch a thirty-minute train ride into Edinburgh.

"How did you get into digital, Phil?" I ask. "Are you an early adopter?"

"I feel like I was both an early adopter and a late adopter of digital," he tells me. "I'm certainly not one of those people, of whom there are several at Blonde, who were on the Internet from day one and who have every computer and game console they ever owned stashed in the attic. Nor have I ever been a gamer.

"That said, I think I probably am an early adopter compared to many advertising people of my generation. We started Blonde in 2006, the year I turned forty. I'd been in the business for eighteen years by that time, and I know that a lot of my peers either consciously or subconsciously buried their heads in the sand about the whole digital thing, assuming that they were too old, or that they were too late into it, or both."

The train crosses the iconic Forth Road Bridge again, and I admire the sunrise over the ocean.

When we arrive at Edinburgh station, there's another fifteen-minute walk uphill to the office. Phil is in good shape, as evidenced by his swift pace and lack of huffing as we head up the hill. Even with an hour's commute, he woke up early this morning to go for a run. Despite my long stride, I have to work to keep up with him. All of this traveling has let me get lax with my workout routine.

We walk with the ancient city and the peak of Arthur's Seat to our backs, toward the office. Half of Edinburgh is modern while the other half is preserved as the medieval city it once was.

We come upon a café that appears to do mostly take-away business. "Let's stop here and pick up coffees," Phil says.

"Ooh, and a sausage roll?" I ask. I have no willpower when I'm visiting the Kingdom.

A friendly guy at the counter quickly delivers small paper-wrapped parcels into our hands. They sure know how to cram meat into intestine casings in this part of the world.

With brekkie and coffee in hand, we arrive at the office, and Phil puts me at the table facing him in an open-plan space. His desk is all about work, with no room for family snapshots. He's decided to approach my visit as an opportunity for partnership as opposed to internship, so I'll be working alongside him on all of his projects as an extra pair of hands.

As we finish our coffees, I ask Phil more about his background. Phil had mentioned when we first met that he had studied chemical engineering at university. "So how did you made the switch from engineering to advertising?" I ask.

"I realized a bit late that I didn't want to be a scientist," he tells me. So he sought an escape hatch by following the lead of a fellow engineering student who, looking to avoid a career in science, was putting an advertising book together.

Captivated by the idea of the advertising business, Phil managed to get on the grad scheme at BBH London where he then worked for five and a half years, learning the craft of client handling.

During that time, he proposed to his school sweetheart, Rachel, and the two decided that London wasn't where they wanted to raise a family. Instead, eighteen years ago, they chose to move to Scotland, where Phil joined a little agency called Leith and fast-tracked his way to managing director. Then, five years ago, when it became clear that digital was not going away, he helped set up Blonde as a sister company to Leith. While setting up Blonde, he realized he loved strategy more than the MD role; he'd crossed the chasm from classic brand builder to modern digital doula.

"With hindsight," he tells me, "I was bored after eighteen years in traditional agencies. Digital came along at just the right time for me.

"The first thing I learned was how much I didn't know about the technology side of things. But pretty quickly I learned enough to understand that certain ideas have technical implications that have to be checked before presenting to the client. It didn't take me long to learn enough to stay out of trouble. And my engineer training means that I'm hardwired to want to know how things work. So rather than trying to cover for my ignorance, I embraced it and dived in. I deliberately sat myself within the dev team so as to learn by osmosis, and I asked lots of naive questions.

"I also learned that not many people in the nascent digital industry had the first idea about strategy. And, whilst there were lots of talented designers, not many people understood how to brief and evaluate conceptual creativity. So I was able to make valuable contributions from day one that actually differentiated the agency and helped us win new clients."

Blonde has a mix of Scottish, UK, and European clients, and their approach to brand strategy parallels many of the front-runners of brand strategy today: Simon Sinek starts with *why*, Ty Montague creates a brand's metastory, and Phil, too, has set up a simple framework . . . he starts with what he calls a "commercially valuable statement of purpose."

"It's a really bad disease in digital to do stuff for the sake of it rather than serving a commercial purpose," he says. "It's also a function of the fact that a lot of clients tend to brief digital agencies in a downstream sort of way. So a typical brief specifies a solution: We want a Facebook page, or we want a microsite."

To combat those impulses, he gets his team to start with the question "How can we_____ so that_____." For example, How can we influence a desired behavior so that we achieve a commercial outcome?

One rule Phil enforces is that his team is not allowed to use the words "engage," "engaging," or "engagement" for the desired behavior.

"It means everything, and therefore it means nothing," he says. "It's not a metric with any sort of standard. It lacks precision." (See *The Power of a Clever Name*)

I find it interesting that many people are coming to the same conclusion that brands must be driven from a statement of purpose. This is evidence of multiples: several people concluding similar theories separately. In practice, a purpose statement leads to brand actions, not just to communications. I think this is the most important place to start with any brand, because it combats the creation of digital nonsense, or, as Tim Malbon aptly put it, "filling the digital landfill with bollocks."

It also goes back to the metaphor of "brand as game show host" I shared at Hyper Island. People don't want to share their story of triumph with, say, a toilet tissue brand. And yet so many brands keep asking.

FAST AND WEIRD

Because of the Fringe Festival, I quickly realized that Edinburgh isn't such an out-of-the-way place after all. During this month, the world comes to Edinburgh. The Festival makes Edinburgh unique—even more so than haggis, the culinary treat that mixes offal and oatmeal and is infamous here. The Fringe Festival, the world's largest arts festival, is comprised of events spanning all sorts of comedy and theater productions big and small. The Turing Festival (which is focused on technology) and the Edinburgh Book Festival (I'll let you guess what that's about) also pile on their events each August just to make it extra hard to get a hotel room. It's a strategist's wet dream to attend because you're surrounded by the latest endeavors in several fields.

Phil has planned for us to attend several events while I'm here, and he'd even sent me a Google Docs spreadsheet prior to my arrival to prove his diligence. Having arrived mid-Festival, I benefit from the many people who have already sniffed and sorted out the painfully obscure from the award-winning performances.

In fact, Blonde built a handy site that ranks the performances by using sentiment analysis of any tweets mentioning Fringe shows. They named it Ed Twinge. This type of platform-thinking—creating a product that will only grow in relevance and usefulness over time—is a critical distinction between platform-thinking and campaign-thinking, where you create something to be relevant only for a brief moment in time. I've seen a lot of criticism (especially in Leif Abraham's book *Madison Valley*) that contends agencies don't know how to think in terms of platforms and products, and that sticking to the small world of campaigns will limit and shrink the relevance of agencies. And then I see an example like Ed Twinge, and it gives me some hope that agencies do have the patience and are willing to develop this type of know-how too.

On my first afternoon in the office, we cut loose early to see Ben Hammersley, futurist, writer, and former editor at large for *Wired UK*, speak at the Book Festival. From our cramped, uncomfortably erect metal chairs, sitting side by side with mostly retirees (are these the only people who can attend book events on a Monday afternoon?), we listen to Hammersley bleakly proffer that many professions will soon be replaced by algorithms. From behind his substantial mustache, he tells us, "As Moore's law carries on and computing power increases, we won't be able to turn off modernity, and we might be overrun with uncertainty at first."

But fret not, he tells us as he reveals there's hope. We can expect to cut through complexity, and he imagines a day when the "boring bits" of our work become easy—we'll no longer be enslaved to spreadsheets, and we'll be able to focus on the fun stuff of ideas and creativity.

He shared an intriguing story of a famous twentieth-century military strategist, US Air Force Colonel John Boyd, who studied dogfights to determine how jet pilots make decisions and create situations that are ultimately successful. He found that pilots would continually go through four different phases: observe, orient, decide, and act. After observing what the enemy is doing, a pilot uses his expertise to orient the enemy's behavior with what he expects to happen next; then he decides what to do and executes that decision. The entire sequence then begins again and repeats in a loop. This is now known as the "Boyd loop" or "OODA loop."

It might seem that Boyd was merely stating the obvious, but the brilliance arises from the strategies he discovered to upset an enemy's OODA loop. The first strategy is to be quicker. If you take less time than your competitor, you can thwart their next move and essentially short-circuit their loop. The second strategy is to be weird. If your opponent is observing you and trying to orient to your intentions, doing things he doesn't expect will throw him off. He can't guess what you will do next when you've made your next moves too difficult to predict.

As we listen, it occurs to me that understanding the Boyd loop and the insights of using speed and weirdness to your advantage aren't just for military application; they're just as beneficial in the business world. Aren't all forms of "the new" about taking advantage of speed and breaking with conventions? And today, the best companies adopt the ethos of perpetual beta, which is really just a handle for putting the Boyd loop into practice.

"I loved the Boyd loop story," I tell Phil as we stroll back down the hill after the talk. "It seems like a handy example to share with clients when they're uneasy with an idea that's out of their comfort zone."

"I like it, too," he says, "particularly because it aligns with our approach at Blonde, which I've been articulating as 'providing ingenious digital solutions to commercial problems.' The acid test of ingeniousness is that an idea appears obvious after we've presented it but not before, like, *Why hasn't anyone thought of this before?* We like to be able to point to some aspect of each project that was ingenious: the strategy, a creative idea, a new use of existing technology, a clever UX, a few elegant lines of code that make something very difficult possible."

Creating a product out of the sentiment analysis of Festival-related tweets certainly qualifies as ingenious—a word I love—and I can't wait to see more of Blonde's ingenious examples.

THE ART OF THE LEDE

Phil's long commute turns out to be a gift. The train cars are not so crowded as to prohibit an open laptop, and so this portion of the journey allows for reviewing Phil's past conference presentations and case studies of his past work. As we review, a theme emerges of how a little forward thinking can hugely impact the ability to learn from marketing experiments.

On our Thursday evening ride, Phil shares a poignant example from Blonde's work with IRN-BRU, the fizzy, electric-orange soda I mentioned earlier known for its outrageous ads and the strapline "IRN-BRU gets you through." (As a side note, Scotland is the only country in the world where Coke or another Coca-Cola product isn't the most popular soda.) Blonde was recently brought in to support a new TV spot (made by the agency Leith) that built on the long-running campaign where people drink IRN-BRU to cope with embarrassing social situations. The advert featured a pair of new parents in the hospital welcoming their baby daughter. The dad asks, "What are we going to call her?" to which the mum replies, "Fanny, I want to call her Fanny." Now, in the UK, "fanny" is a slang term for a woman's nether regions, which is also why the American name for a bum bag ("fanny pack") is endlessly humorous to Brits. The dad reacts, "You *cannot* call her Fanny," shaking his head as he reaches for an IRN-BRU.

But after he drinks the magic elixir, he starts nodding in agreement. "Fanny, eh? I like it! It's unusual. Unique!" His mother-in-law on the other side of the hospital bed says, "Mum's a Fanny. Granny was a Fanny. She'll be joining a long line of Fannys," as she proudly holds up a homemade sweater that says "Fanny."

The dad drinks more IRN-BRU, nods again and says, "Aye, it's good to keep up tradition." We close on an end card with the line "IRN-BRU gets you through."

Blonde's brief from IRN-BRU was to enhance the campaign with digital components. They began their ideation with the belief that this commercial was the closest thing to a spreadable social media "sure thing" as it gets.

Rather than release the new spot on TV in a typical way, Blonde did something weird: They created an ingenious plan for distribution, one that had never been used before. They decided that one fan would be given the privilege of sharing the YouTube link with the world for the first time, before the spot ever ran on broadcast. To be selected for this honor, a lottery was announced on Twitter with a one-word tweet: "IRNBRUFanny.com."

When experimenting, it's exceedingly difficult to know if things will work, but it's imperative that you measure the results so that when things *do* go well, you can use the successes to learn from and to build momentum toward a virtuous cycle with clients.

"It's deceptively simple," Phil says, "because if you get the statement of purpose right, what success looks like should be quite obvious. Good evaluation is a craft skill. There are so many vanity metrics, but just because you can measure something doesn't mean it's telling you something important. It's a sort of editorial skill about what matters and what doesn't. I ask my team to think ahead to six months in, or to when a campaign has run its course. You have to imagine the story you want to tell of how your efforts have performed. Then it's more clear, the sorts of data you'd need to build your story, and you make damn sure they're being collected, whether that means they must be built into the code or the client needs to pay for some research. You have to think about evaluation from a storytelling perspective and predict what tools you'll need to tell that story."

Phil's take on evaluation and metrics reminds me of the journalistic principle of crafting your lede, the introduction to an article designed to draw the reader in a teaser format. It includes just enough to contain the essence of the story and make the reader care. The lede for this IRN-BRU effort might be "Scotland's most popular beverage, IRN-BRU, is famous for its uncommonly funny adverts, and now it will be known for releasing them using uncommonly clever digital pathways. Their latest spot, "Fanny," reached a million YouTube views in less than a month."

With this endgame in mind, Blonde carried out the campaign.

First, Rachel Orr—aka @larachie, a twenty-three-year-old student from Motherwell with 153 Twitter followers—won the initial lottery. Before she was given the link, Blonde did a little profile boosting from the IRN-BRU feed, encouraging fans to follow her. They also instigated an underground competition among the top Scottish influencers on Twitter. If the influencers followed Rachel and retweeted the advert link when she tweeted it, they'd find out the impact of their individual influence on the shared link. Blonde analyzed evidence of how the tweets spread and used data visualization tools to reveal the winner.

Within twenty-four hours of Rachel sharing the link, the ad had been viewed 100,000 times. The analytics revealed that a couple of dozen influencers were responsible for most of those views. This is the "tipping point" effect of word of mouth: a few influencers reaching the masses. But after that first day, a very different dynamic emerged when those masses of people began sharing the link with their family and friends. While not influential to thousands of people, this tier of "sharers" each enlisted a few additional viewers, otherwise known as organic word of mouth. As Paul Adams, author of the book *Grouped: How Small Groups of Friends Are the Key to Influence on the Social Web*, says, "The people who do have influence over our behavior are usually the people who are emotionally closest to us." This was proved out over the next twenty-one days, as the YouTube views grew from 100,000 to 650,000 due to the activity of lots of small groups of people.

The last factor that propelled the ad to over a million views was a good old-fashioned TV buy. "Fanny" ran just a few times during the European Football Championships, and those placements were responsible for another 300,000 views in just forty-eight hours, pushing the views to over one million.

"There's a lot of misguided 'either/or' talk when it comes to social media and broadcast media," Phil told me. "This case hopefully shows that an 'and' approach is far more effective than an 'or' one."

My notebook is packed with so many good lessons from this case: Begin with the end in mind. Influencers are helpful, but only up to a point. Many small networks trump a few influencers alone. And last, think "and" not "or" when it comes to the power of social media and broadcast channels.

EVERY DAY I'M SHUFFLIN'

At the weekend, Phil and Rachel pack all of us girls into the SUV, and we head into town. As opposed to Blonde, which is located on the more modern side of Edinburgh, the Fringe Festival occurs on the medieval side. We walk uphill on ancient cobblestones, past a castle. Phil points out the pub where J.K. Rowling wrote *Harry Potter*.

Phil has scoured the Fringe offerings looking for family-friendly shows that will delight all of us. We start with *The Scottish Falsetto Sock Puppet Theatre,* one man's identity crisis delivered through his sock-covered hands. His falsetto Scottish accent comes from somewhere behind the tartan curtains that frame his miniature stage. It's fast-paced and silly. We all enjoy it.

After lunch, we file in for *The Snail and the Whale*, which is a small stage musical targeted to the ten-and-under crowd. The entirety of the show is sung in rhyming couplets to a hypnotic melody. So of course we satirize and remix the rhymes to the same melody the whole way home.

In the evening, the girls spark up *Dance Dance Revolution* on the Wii in the family room. Madeleine and I nail some ABBA, and then Molly, Lois, and Penny demonstrate perfect choreography to Katy Perry and Rihanna. But the real showstopper is the surprise performance Rachel and Phil put on when they select LMFAO's "Party Rock Anthem." Once they start "shufflin'," tears are streaming down my face and the girls are cracking up.

On Sunday afternoon, I offer to make tacos and guacamole for dinner.

"I know you're from Texas," Phil says, "but I think my guacamole is pretty good. Care to make a wager?"

We pick out our ingredients at the market together. Phil remarks that, given it's such a small town, someone will likely make a comment to Rachel about him shopping with some mystery woman.

Back at the house, we get to chopping. When we're both finished, Phil sets his completed guacamole on the table next to mine.

"Oh bugger," he says.

My guacamole, the native Texan's guacamole, is lively, chunky, and green. His, on the other hand, is creamy and ever so slightly brown.

"You don't stand a chance," I laugh, as we both take pictures and upload them to Facebook.

We then invite the girls to the kitchen table to judge.

"I rove guacamole!" announces Madeleine with mouth full.

"Dad, I don't think guacamole is supposed to be brown," Penny says.

The girls unanimously agree I'm the winner. Phil concedes the showdown, shaking his head. "I should have gone chunky."

This weekend has impressed upon me that it is absolutely possible to stay current in the demanding, ever-changing work challenges that the digital landscape presents and still manage to have a vibrant life at home. Perhaps that means choosing a smaller market such as Edinburgh to make that happen, but it certainly doesn't mean sacrificing interesting work or even international brands. If the choice of where to work at the end of this journey is between a company where the glory days are behind it and one that embraces experimentation, I know the right choice for me . . . and I now know that such a company might be hiding in an unexpected city.

SPOILER ALERT

Ed Twinge, the ranking website Blonde built, bestowed the title of "Number One, Must-See Performance" to *The Boy with Tape on His Face*, so Phil planned an evening out for all of the Blonde strategists to see it. If you've never heard of this performer, I highly recommend making an effort to see him, but now I will proceed to describe some of his act, so skip ahead to the next section if you plan to go see him and would prefer not to know.

The Boy, as he calls himself, is a modern mime. Instead of painting his face white, he's covered his mouth with (you guessed it) tape, and he communicates loads with his wide-open eyes. He never makes a sound, and in fact when I saw him speaking in interviews on YouTube afterward, it felt almost sacrilegious. On a nearly empty stage, he silently plays little games and scenes, and you experience just what ingenious means.

For example, one of his first bits has him come out on stage to the tinkling sound of a child's music box. He wears jeans, a T-shirt, a blazer, and a small messenger bag. He removes an old-school leather pilot's hat and goggles from the bag and puts them on. Then he pulls a stool over to the center of the stage. He prepares himself for a moment, and then lies down belly-first on the stool.

The theater floods with Tom Petty's "Free Fallin'," and The Boy comes to life, raising his arms and legs and slowly leaning back and forth, pretending he's just jumped out of a plane. It's unexpected, silly, and delightful.

In another scene, while accordion music plays, he goes out into the audience and picks out a twenty-something guy to join him on stage. The Boy directs his volunteer to stand at the edge of the stage and then takes out two tape measures from his bag. He gives one to his guest while holding the other with two hands, directly in front of his crotch. Then Maria McKee's "Show Me Heaven" from the *Days Of Thunder* soundtrack begins, and he stretches the tape out a couple of feet. The two enter into a silent pissing match, each taking turns and extending their tape measures while the crowd laughs. Finally, the volunteer's tape falls over limply, and the boy admires his work and gloats with his eyes.

Back in Blonde's main conference room the next day, Phil and I discuss how much we loved the performance.

"He's so good at creating different scenes that hang well together," Phil says. "We try to do the same when we're creating content for a brand. We take a brand's core proposition and turn it into consumer-facing content. Again and again and again. That's what we've done with 'The Daylight Project' for Velux. People may only be interested in skylights during a very narrow point in time when they're building or remodeling, but to build awareness of Velux, instead of buying ads, we've built their brand around the positive aspects of bringing daylight into buildings. People are genuinely interested in the effect of sunlight on our productivity or in learning there's a newly discovered cell in the eye that recognizes light and sets our internal clock. Over time, this kind of content will increase the likelihood of many different people stumbling across Velux."

Just like The Boy's content, a brand can create a simple springboard that takes into consideration *What will people find interesting?* You can imagine The Boy working on his material, polishing it for bigger laughs, abandoning some altogether, and having to keep coming up with new stuff to keep audiences coming back. Sounds a lot like creating and learning as you go with branded content.

"You saw the Jay-Z and Tiger Woods infographic, right?" Phil quickly does a Google search and shows me the brilliant infographic titled "Problems."

A basic chart lists Jay-Z's name with ninety-nine gray circles next to it identifying the problems he has *not* had relating to women, and below that Tiger Woods has ninety-nine aqua circles identifying problems he's had relating to women.

"The week this was posted to BuzzFeed," Phil says, "it was the fourth most shared. Why do you think it took off?"

"Well, clearly it was funny and timely . . . but I'm guessing you see more in it than that?"

"You're on to me. This infographic spoke to many communities of interest at once: people who like hip-hop, and Jay-Z in particular; sports and celebrity, Tiger in particular; as well as geeks, dorks, and nerds who like infographics, designers, and data heads. You can imagine people from all those spheres of influence finding a reason to share this. And that's what we try to do with our content strategy. How many spheres of influence might we find a way to be relevant for? Rather than a PR approach of "It's Valentine's Day; think about getting your sweetheart a skylight,' we're thinking about science, psychology, design, life hacking and productivity."

To me, there is a serendipitous parallel between the Fringe Festival exploring the boundaries of performance art and the need for marketers to do the same, exploring the boundaries of what's been done before, to grow brands. With content especially, the push to identify more and more spheres of influence is a brilliant exercise: It helps us to create content that's compelling for users. Thinking in the reverse works too: If we've got a good idea, we can make it better by pressing to identify which additional spheres of influence could enhance it.

KEEP LEARNING

On our last Thursday, we take the train home for the last time together. These two weeks have been chock-full of new experiences and breathtaking scenery. I take in the rolling hills and ocean view, knowing it's going to be all bicycles, canals, and gray skies for me back in Amsterdam.

Thinking about journeys reminds me of an adventure I knew Phil had taken: A few years earlier, he and a few friends participated in an event called the Mongol Rally, an anti-race where the purpose is to drive a shit car from Europe to Mongolia, slowly, down the road less traveled, preferably breaking down often so you can have real adventures and learn to summon your wits.

When I ask Phil for more details, he looks off into the distance as if remembering a harrowing scene, and then says, "I saw a donkey do a cartwheel after being hit by a Mercedes in Uzbekistan."

I'm not sure if I should laugh or be horrified. "That is certainly a unique experience," I say. "But overall, do you think the rally made you a better strategist?"

"I don't know how driving a secondhand ambulance bought on eBay across Central Asia made me a better strategist, but I'm sure it did," he says. "I think the importance of curiosity as a trait in strategists is overstated. It's important to fill your head with fresh material and influences, but it's more important to have the kind of brain that puts things together in original and relevant ways. I'm very taken with the idea of Diagonal Thinking. That's an applied skill. Anyone can be curious."

That we must think deductively *and* inductively, or linearly *and* laterally, is the idea behind Diagonal Thinking. The Institute of Practitioners in Advertising, or IPA, a professional organization in the UK, built a site found at diagonalthinking.co.uk where you can assess your own abilities.

Phil is often filling his mind with new things in order to think diagonally.

"I learn every day," he says. "Digital and social are not as powerful as traditional advertising when it comes to building consumer brands, but they can solve a much greater variety of problems, and so the intellectual challenges are more varied. The move to Blonde has refreshed and reinvigorated me. I feel more interested and more useful at forty-six than I did at twenty-six."

I really adore working with Phil, not least because he's a committed lifelong learner. As he told me when I asked if I could share example cases and presentations of his, "It's not like it's the last idea I'm ever going to have. I feel like it's always better to be open than closed." I wish I could stay and work like this all the time. (See *Strategic Duos*)

Phil's talent brings to mind a pitch I once worked on for a tire brand in the US. To research the project, I went to an event called Hot Import Nights to interview some "tuners"—people who modify their cars, not unlike the kind you see in *The Fast and the Furious*. One guy taught me the taxonomy of this subculture: On the one hand, there are those who aim for flash—those who have giant spoilers designed for intergalactic travel and paint jobs that would make a blind man cringe—and on the other hand, a more subtle group, to which he belonged, who focus on what's under the hood. Their goal is to create a "sleeper"—a car that appears relatively normal but will smoke you at any stoplight when they pull away. That's the kind of strategist, and person, Phil is. You have no idea how good he is. What I learned from spending time with him was the importance of staying on the fringe of what we know in our work, not only because it's more interesting and satisfying but also because the lifeblood of a brand is found in imagination and experimentation. It takes a willingness to jump wholeheartedly into every aspect of what's new—in this case, digital marketing—rather than bowing out and sticking to what we know best. I now see that an experimental approach coupled with a strong foundation in brand and communications hones our ability to create powerful digital work.

the power of
A CLEVER NAME

BY PHIL ADAMS

We use different tools at Blonde that we've given funky names to put people at ease. For example—and I didn't come up with this, Gavin MacDonald did—the "Totally Tough Tone of Voice Challenge" is an activity designed to get beyond the typical unholy trinity of "authentic, confident, and fun" that so many brands aspire to be. The rule is you cannot suggest a word where the opposite would not be a viable choice for a brand. Can you imagine an inauthentic, anxious and boring brand? Well, sure, several insurance brands come to mind, but they haven't achieved that tone deliberately.

Clients utterly hate this exercise. It's hard. But we always get someplace good. You don't have to impose your view on everyone. It's so important to bring everyone on a journey together.

Another exercise we call "What's your 4:48 Psychosis?" It's named after the play *4.48 Psychosis* by Sarah Kane, which she titled as such because this was so often the time she saw when she turned over and read her digital clock while suffering from insomnia: 4:48 a.m. So it's really a variation on the theme of what keeps you awake at night.

We also play a game called "Henry II", who is alleged to have said, "Who will rid me of this troublesome priest?" referring to Thomas Becket, the Archbishop of Canterbury, who excommunicated Henry II's son, Henry the Young King. In this game, we're trying to frame the problem as something we want to eliminate or have taken out.

STRATEGIC
duos

BY PHIL ADAMS

As luck would have it, a couple of juicy strategy projects landed in the office a couple of days before Heather's plane landed at Edinburgh Airport. This meant that Heather and I could properly work together. She could see my approach to strategy in action, rather than have it described in theory. And I got a glimpse of what it must be like for creative teams to work together on briefs.

This probably shouldn't have been a revelation, but it was.

Obviously I work with other strategists all the time. We help each other out. We share ideas. We give advice. We act as editors for each other's work. We collaborate. The daily functioning of a strategy department.

But working with Heather was different.

The daily functioning of a strategy department is collaborative, but it is broken into individual work streams. People help each other out but each individual is ultimately responsible for his or her unique to-do list.

Heather and I had a single, identical to-do list.

We were the strategy equivalent of art director and copywriter. "My" work was better by any measure as a result. And it was delivered more quickly.

Which has me thinking.

Could a strategy department be structured like a creative department? Strategic duos? Identical to-do lists? Better output, arrived at more quickly?

And this line of thinking raises all sorts of interesting questions. How and when would these pairs form, especially if yours were the only agency operating in this manner?

Strategists wouldn't come out of college in pairs. So you'd need to have a system for recruiting and pairing up. How would that work, given the various vocational and personal levels on which compatibility would need to be achieved? It would be like intellectual tissue matching.

And even if strategists did come in pairs, how would they feel about going in pairs too? Would they, could they, move from agency to agency as a twosome? That's the norm for creatives, but it would be a new paradigm (obligatory wanky strategist term) for strategy.

Creatives get offered new jobs on the basis of a joint reputation earned with their partners. Maybe that dynamic could work for strategists too. Strategist X and Strategist Y earn a reputation for great strategy, stimulating great creative work, winning lots of pitches, great client relationships at Agency Z. From the outside looking in, it is impossible to tell which, if either, is contributing more to this reputation. And so they are headhunted as a pair. Put like that it doesn't sound too far-fetched actually.

LEAD culture

SUZANNE POWERS

Crispin Porter + Bogusky | London

chapter
SIX

"You will never influence the world by trying to be like it."
– Sean McCabe

This chapter of the journey took me to the Crispin Porter + Bogusky advertising agency in London, which was a homecoming of sorts because I'd spent a year and a half as an employee there in 2007 and 2008, albeit in their Miami office. I specifically wanted to return because it was at CP+B that I'd been most intellectually challenged and where hard work seemed to pay off the most. Great ideas happened more easily and were produced more often than at other places I've worked. I wanted to build on what I'd learned from my first stint at CP+B, to deconstruct both my experience and their ongoing success (for example, they've won more Grand Prix at Cannes than any other company: nine since 2001).

I targeted my host Suzanne Powers deliberately. She'd joined CP+B as chief strategy officer after I'd left, and though she was receptive to the project when we chatted on Skype, it was difficult to coordinate schedules with her because she's rarely in one place for two weeks straight. Although she lives in New York with her twin eleven-year-old sons Nate and Gordon and her partner Steve, the CEO of a media firm, she leads an itinerant life across offices in Los Angeles, Boulder, Miami, and London, not to mention she also attends client meetings and pitches that could be anywhere.

Suzanne, forty-something and petite with shoulder-length brown hair, is Canadian by birth but has strong family ties to Los Angeles. She also has a long list of seemingly unrelated early jobs prior to working in advertising that I could really identify with: While still in college, she taught preschool where dealing with privileged parents gave her valuable skills for future focus-group moderation.

Next, she wrote press releases and hounded radio DJs to get them to mention the comedians represented by the small PR firm she worked for, which taught her the art of grabbing someone's attention. Then she ran a gift wrapping station while working for a shopping mall/retail marketing company, and actually got to hire the mall Santa and his elves, giving her an entrée into staffing a team.

"Are you kidding?" I ask when she tells me about this last job. I can't imagine such a successful woman working in Santa's workshop.

"It's not a joke!" she tells me. "Out of fear of repeating the same seasonal shift again, I called in sick one day, bought a copy of *Adweek*, and found a 'Help Wanted' listing for a strategist. It said the current strategist would leave big shoes to fill, so I sketched a shoe and put my resume in the middle with a letter. I got the job."

"Not everyone makes it to chief strategy officer, though. How did that happen?"

"Well, that first shop was Lord, Dentsu & Partners in LA. My boss quit soon after I came on, and I took her job. Then I spent two years running strategy at Suissa Miller, followed by an amazing ten years running global businesses at TBWA\Chiat\Day. Chuck Porter came along and wooed me away to join CP+B and plan further global expansion. How could I say no?"

After just one Skype, I was sucked in by Suzanne's high energy. And given her role at CP+B, I anticipated getting a stronger grip on how CP+B is so successful at morphing pop culture in the service of brands. After all this additional time and compounded success, I wondered just how the agency had changed.

Which brings us to the present day and our rendezvous in London, where Suzanne is in the midst of a pitch. Her partner Steve is English and happens to keep a flat in London, so we are simply carrying out this experiment at her home away from home.

I already know London pretty well from years of quick business trips, weekend visits, and commutes for freelance work. There are two worlds in London: the world above ground and the world below. I always get a good reintroduction to both of them after landing at City Airport. This time I take the Overground, which delivers me to the Underground, where I transfer at Bank to the Northern Line and then—go toward the light!—emerge at King's Cross station, where the London office of CP+B is a block away.

PATTERN RECOGNITION

As an observer looking for the secret sauce that makes CP+B tick, I wish I were able to give all the employees a wearable device to track every word they speak and do a content analysis of what they talk about. Because even in the first day, I can tell that "culture" seems to be vital to getting work done at CP+B.

I hear the word "culture" so much that an outsider might assume it's a linguistic crutch. But on the contrary, understanding and shifting culture is a fundamental philosophical mainstay at CP+B.

Now, I'm not talking about corporate culture or high culture like fine art. I'm using the word in its broader sense to capture the beliefs and behaviors of a group of people. This can then be sliced into smaller divisions such as "American culture" or "pop culture" or more specific groups such as "running culture." It's one thing to identify different subcultures and articulate where they've been and where they are now . . . or now . . . or now, but it takes a totally different set of skills to actually shape culture as a future-focused endeavor.

Trying to understand where this philosophy of shifting culture came from, I dug into old articles online and found CP+B's prophetesque, long-time leader Alex Bogusky once brilliantly put it like this:

> *Generally culture is going multiple directions at any one time. And pop-culture, specifically, is always having this conversation with itself about where to go. A lot of advertisers talk about relevance, but they never define it. What is relevant? To me, being relevant is to be in the conversation that pop culture is having about any particular topic. But if you're going to be relevant, you're going to be somewhat controversial, because culture hasn't really decided, okay, this is the direction now. And so, you have to be . . . okay with the heat that comes with being relevant.*

CP+B is no stranger to heat. I'm thinking in particular of when they used the magic of CGI to bring Orville Redenbacher back from the dead to shill microwave popcorn. That caused a stir. Or the Jell-O social media campaign "Fun My Life," where the brand tried to hijack the profane #fml hashtag and offer free Jell-O to the discontented. Many Twitter users saw this as making light of some people's legitimate suffering and thus considered it in poor taste.

Sure, sometimes ideas backfire, but on balance CP+B has had far more hits than whiffs. The Twelpforce campaign for Best Buy is a noteworthy example: It won the Titanium Grand Prix at Cannes in 2010, and it was the idea that unleashed the army of Best Buy staff with technical expertise onto Twitter to answer problems and questions posed on the site. Why was the campaign so popular? Twitter's novelty, coupled with the live-chat-style customer service delivered by real people

(Best Buy's key point of difference), helped customers to navigate a world where electronics are becoming more complex and pervasive necessities rather than nice-to-haves. As is always the case, an idea like this that was once revolutionary now seems pedestrian.

CP+B widened people's perspective of food beyond the predominant "organic" and "artisanal" fixation at the time by suggesting a need for foods that offer some joy in life (like Jell-O). They also showed that choosing electronics can be easier when you pose your questions to an expert (like Best Buy) instead of just trusting anonymous online reviews. These examples and others have proved that CP+B's superpower is charting cultural courses for brands.

ACTING ON CULTURE

Early in my weeklong stay, Suzanne and I walk a few blocks from the office to get some lunch from the food trucks that gather behind the nearby train station. It's cold, and I can see my breath as we chat about taking chances to shape culture.

"If we could scientifically predict cultural traction," Suzanne tells me, "Hollywood would never have a flop, there would be a Grammy on every musician's mantel, there would never be a 'sales rack' in a clothing store, and we'd all be the founders of successful start-ups. But it clearly doesn't work like that. And what CP+B does better than anyone is attempt to articulate where things might be heading and then help a brand choose a possible future to invest in."

What's most interesting to me about this stance is how it marries uncertainty with decisiveness. I've always been a very decisive person, to the extent that I get a bit murdery when faced with bureaucracies that thrive on indecision. At times, it's seemed as though a career in the advertising agency world was the perfect torture designed just for me. But it wasn't until I went to CP+B where there was a bias toward action that I finally found my groove and felt like I'd broken out of the torture chamber.

My conversation with Suzanne reminded me of philosopher Ruth Chang, who specializes in understanding decision making. Chang brilliantly articulates the distinction between easy and hard choices. In an easy choice, there's clearly a better alternative, and the decision can be taken swiftly. Easy choices are those where the decision criterion is quantitative: One alternative takes more time or less time, or is more expensive or less expensive, or any number of other metrics. You simply decide which metrics you will base your decision on, review the data, and make your choice.

Hard choices, by comparison, are those where the selection criteria depend on principles and values. For example, say you are faced with the choice between two jobs. One may pay more than the other, but it may still not be the best choice for *you*. If you value living in the country over living in the city, or having a mentor to learn from, or being challenged in your work, you might place higher value on the job that provides whichever criterion is most important to you, even if it means lower pay.

"We tend to assume that scientific thinking holds the key to everything of importance in our world," Chang says, "but the world of value is different from the world of science. . . . We shouldn't assume that the world of *is*—of lengths and weights—has the same structure as the world of *ought*—of what we should do."

This I interpret to mean that we too often try to apply science to all of our decisions, thus implicitly cramming them into the "easy" bucket where there is a right answer.

She goes on to make a powerful point, something I've thought for many years but never heard articulated: "Hard choices are hard because there is no best option."

The "best" option is ultimately an assertion of principles. In my experience, most companies are reluctant to assert themselves, especially once they reach full-grown bureaucracy status. But outrageous success never comes from sitting on our hands.

Chang calls out such hand-sitters, reminding us of the label we have for people who fail to make a call in life: We call them drifters. Sadly, that epithet strikes me as highly appropriate to characterize a large swath of brands that try to make every decision an "easy" quantitative one. It's this seductive red-herring logic that emerges from an ability to measure far more than we ever could before.

But I wonder, what's the point of coming up with strategic platforms and ideas for brands if they aren't put out into the world? If you believe that culture is a powerful force for a brand, that it is the primordial ooze from which brands evolve, then any given idea has a shelf life. So even if bureaucratic drifter brands are willing to pay for the meetings, research, and concepting, should we as practitioners be paying for their reluctance with our time?

It depends on how much we value money over seeing good work alive in the wild. It's our own hard choice to make.

I share my thoughts on Chang's ideas with Suzanne, and ask what she thinks about drifter brands.

"Whether it's brands or people," she says, "life either happens *to* them, and they just get in a cycle of merely reacting, or they function more intentionally, with purpose."

We choose some take-away paella from a truck called Jamon Jamon to bring back to the office. The box of food warms my gloved hands as we walk and talk over the roar of a passing train on the tracks just below us.

"I think that's what I most enjoyed about working with Burger King at the time," I say. "They were the opposite of a drifter brand. I'm not sure what I'd call that. An action brand maybe?"

"Yeah, I like that. Intentions are only as good as the actions we put behind them," Suzanne says, "hence the saying 'actions speak louder than words,' or at least that's how I interpret it."

"I think this is why the brand-purpose philosophy of communications has gained a lot of traction in the marketing world but doesn't always work in practice." I'm thinking of the countless decks I've seen full of Simon Sinek's Golden Circle, urging brands to start from their why, their reason to exist, instead of what they make and how they make it. "We end up citing the same usual suspects like Apple and Nike because they really seem to act deliberately from a place of purpose, but the vast majority of brands seem to fail to put a purpose into practice."

Suzanne nods as we turn the corner back toward the office. "It's been really interesting working pre-recession and post-recession. Pre-recession, it was more thoughtful. We crafted a vision or mission or whatever and operated from there, pushing out to the world. Post-recession, we react and hope those reactions push us forward. I'm generalizing, of course, but I think operating in a climate of fear has damaged folks."

Operating in a climate of fear, as Suzanne observes, seems to result in needier brands: brands that insist that the features they offer and how they can make you feel will change your life. They have an answer to every barrier a potential customer might raise, but they lack a point of view.

I leave this conversation with a sense that only confident brands make the hard choice to have both a point of view and the courage to act on it.

CODIFYING CULTURAL STRATEGY

In preparing for my visit, I reviewed the two books written about "the factory," as CP+B refers to itself. Of note is the vast portfolio of early work that the company collected (along with co-author Warren Berger) and shared in the massive tome *Hoopla*, published in 2006. The cover of the book was made out of sandpaper with the flippant intention of grabbing some of the reader's skin cells so that he might be cloned when science caught up to such a sci-fi possibility. This feature is a sort of stunt that parallels what is found throughout the book: remarkable examples of advertising created by CP+B. Their work offers proof that Seth Godin was on to something with his assertions in *Purple Cow*: We'd never comment on a brown cow, but a purple one? *That's* a reason to talk. Businesses should make it their business to create more purple cows.

CP+B's launch of the Mini Cooper in the US, for example, deliberately took on the dominant American car culture of big SUVs at a time when gasoline was a dollar a gallon by offering a view of the world where smaller is better. America was charmed by stunts like posters displaying the new Mini comically juxtaposed next to oversized newspaper vending machines stating "Makes everything else seem a little too big."

Seeing outrageously successful campaign after campaign in this book did give me a sense of what crafting a cultural strategy entails, but it left me wanting a clear articulation of how to go about crafting a culturally driven strategy.

The other book is *Baked In,* co-authored by Alex Bogusky and John Winsor (head of the cultural and business insights group at the time), and published in 2010. This slimmer book made the case for CP+B's brand-invention discipline under the premise that more innovative, better-designed, culturally relevant products trump great marketing for average products any day of the week. Reading it gave me the sense that Alex and John were finding more satisfaction in crafting brands and products from scratch than from slogging through campaign creation with risk-averse clients. They mentioned the importance of analyzing culture in broad terms in order to improve and invent timely products and services.

The lack of "how-to" in these books pushed me to reread one more book, *Cultural Strategy* by Douglas Holt and Douglas Cameron, published in 2012. Holt and Cameron don't have anything to do with CP+B, but in reading what they wrote, I finally got the sense it was possible to codify the philosophy and method of crafting culture-shifting strategies. And that CP+B isn't the only company trying to build a business around shifting culture.

This book is more academic than your typical business book, and you have to get used to their lingo because they discuss concepts as yet unnamed in the business vernacular. The key thrust of their work is that cultural innovations exist and can be just as powerful as the better-mousetrap variety of innovations. They define a cultural innovation as a potent new cultural viewpoint, a leading-edge ideology that, from their perspective, society is hankering for. They carefully deconstruct the history of Nike, Starbucks, Jack Daniel's, Ben & Jerry's, and several other brands to prove that in each case, success was forged because of a radical ideology expressed through distinctive advertising and customer touch points (for example, retail environments).

After studying these historical powerhouse brands, Holt and Cameron applied their worldview under their company, Cultural Strategy Group, with their own clients including Clearblue Pregnancy Tests and Fat Tire Beer. Though smaller and less prominent than, say, Nike, the results they've achieved with these partners is proof that rooting a brand strategy in culture can be an advantage.

What really rang true for me was their condemnation of what they call "sciency" marketing. It comes back to Chang's belief that we try to cram our decisions into the "easy" category at every opportunity. Because people can rate which product features and benefits they find most appealing, brands fall into the trap of "benefits slugfests," each one claiming ever more trivial points of difference in hopes of differentiation. I recently saw an ad for Trident gum where they were touting their new small container of already unwrapped pieces as the innovative feature we've all been waiting for. It felt very slugfesty to me. Those of us in the business know features can be forever one-upped and outflanked. It's a rookie mistake to build your brand on features alone.

In the nineties, feature-focused ads gave way to emotional branding. The thinking was that if you could just associate the brand with a desirable emotional outcome like confidence, happiness, or control, then success could be yours! Holt and Cameron claim this is another "sciency" trap: the "commodity emotions trap," to be specific. They write, "In practice, the result is simply to push for vague abstractions that hold a negligible value for consumers," and that building a brand on features and emotional benefits implies that "marketing is about embedding associations between brand and valued benefits in consumers' minds." In their estimation, focusing so heavily on customer perceptions is akin to having a massive blind spot for the opportunities that historical changes in society reveal.

While there is no step-by-step methodology expressed in any of the books I've mentioned, the level of detail in *Cultural Strategy* meant I could reverse-engineer Holt and Cameron's approach in order to create my own methodology for cultural strategies: First, I would gather all the communications in a category to determine what conventions are true for that category. Second, I'd interrogate the history of the category and brand, looking for truths that might be powerful. Third, I'd analyze what I call the primordial ooze of culture, looking for societal thinking and behavior that's still nascent and undecided. These are the clues that lead to unique cultural ideologies. The last step would be to choose and articulate one ideology that the brand should take on as their meaningful stand in the world.

The trick is that, though I've laid them out linearly, these are not steps that follow one after the other. The work of gathering and synthesizing conventions, history, and cultural clues ought to happen simultaneously. Making new connections among what emerges in that analysis is a brand-navigation exercise, which includes triangulation and the charting of a possible strategic direction toward brand growth. The ability to see different possible directions for a brand, to me, is a magical feeling. It's what makes strategizing the best gig.

AN ADVENTUROUS BRAND INVENTION

Suzanne and I talk about culture throughout my visit, and one afternoon she makes the time to sit with me and take me through a case study. We sit at a round table in one of the small conference rooms that overlooks York Way. Red double-decker buses stream down the street below, driving on seemingly the wrong side of the road.

"The work we've done to invent Papa's Pilar is a beautiful example of baked-in strategy and culture shifting," Suzanne says, pulling up a file on her laptop to show me. "Brand invention is so incredible because you are the client *and* the agency. You're making decisions that immediately affect the bottom line, like what the bottle will look like and be made from. The hope is that these brands will be so successful that one day Chuck will wheel a suitcase full of cash into the Agora to share with the whole agency."

We share a knowing laugh, imagining patriarch Chuck Porter as a corporate Santa Claus in the large, open lobby area in the Miami office where all-agency meetings are held.

Papa's Pilar is a brand of rum that CP+B has a one-third stake in. It's just one example of brand invention the agency has invested in.

Suzanne flips through the slides, and the case unfolds to be both beautiful and smart. The brand began as a collaboration among three parties: established rum makers, the Ernest Hemingway heirs, and CP+B. In addition to a start-up budget, the trio had the option to use Hemingway's likeness to create the brand.

The team began by hitting the bottle themselves down in Key West, where Hemingway had worked on *A Farewell to Arms* and spent many a winter to escape the cold. They discovered that Hemingway had led an adventurous life, which he then wrote about. He'd spent time in Paris among the literati of the time, won fishing tournaments in the Caribbean, and hunted game on safari in Africa. CP+B dug so deeply into his life that when they presented their brand strategy to the Hemingway family, Ernest Hemingway's son commented that no film or book had ever done as much to so thoroughly understand his father's vibrant life.

The history of rum proved to be a fascinating source of inputs as well. Rum was invented on the sugarcane plantations of the Caribbean. Its popularity in colonial America drove an increase in the slave trade and a desire for Britain to impose taxes on sugar, which in turn contributed toward the American Revolution. Rum was served at George Washington's inauguration and was the drink of choice during Prohibition. Today, while it can most often be found in fruity, tropical beverages and more often than not served beach-side or poolside, the fact is, rum is a symbol of American rebellion.

In terms of conventions, CP+B reviewed every rum on the market. There were clusters of brands based on strong animals such as Bacardi's bat or the Kraken. Another cluster relied on Caribbean cues such as the Jamaica-based brand Malibu and the pirate-inspired brand Captain Morgan. These brands have cornered the narrow repertoire of clichéd iconic cocktails like daiquiris and mai tais. Most drinkers aren't too savvy about the differences among the spirits.

After all of this analysis, it seemed to CP+B that a brand that championed Hemingway's adventurous spirit would stand out in a Caribbean sea of brands conjuring laid-back relaxation. It would create tension amid the predominant rum culture. (See Tension) The name "Pilar" echoed this opposing worldview of an adventurous spirit, as it was the nickname of one of Hemingway's wives, a character in For Whom the Bell Tolls and also the name of his fishing boat.

The bottle was designed to look like a canteen that you'd take along on an adventure, and the spirit of adventure led to further decisions about how the rum would be sourced and blended. Instead of just one rum maker, Papa's Pilar is sourced from rum makers across the Caribbean. And contrary to conventional rums, which are typically aged only in bourbon barrels, Papa's Pilar is aged in multiple stages in bourbon and port wine barrels and finally finished in Spanish sherry casks. The spirit itself goes on an adventure before ever reaching a glass.

The line "Never a Spectator" is meant to inspire others to seek adventure, which fuels the current cultural interpretation embodied in GoPro–wearing daredevils. The design aesthetic that can be seen on the website uses a color palette of sea glass and African art influences. The brand was further brought to life by small, experiential touches, like installing typewriters that could send tweets in bars that offered Pilar. Creative technologists found a way to strip the guts out of an old typewriter, the very kind Hemingway would have written his novels with, and installed digital components so that it could really send the tweets.

This soup-to-nuts example is just a small hint of the range of expertise that CP+B is developing in-house. When most agencies seem to have a compulsion to recommend TV commercials as the answer for every brand-growth problem, CP+B has a vastly different perspective to draw from; namely, how to lead culture from the product outward.

CULTURE ON THE MOVE

Cultural Strategy authors Holt and Cameron believe that society has a "latent demand for ideology." My first boss at CP+B, Colin Drummond, now CSO for Deutsch, put it better this way: "Culture wants to change."

I'm not sure if I believe that culture is sentient, but there's no doubt that with each passing moment, new minds are born, old minds die, and new ideas are constantly forming. Some ideas catch our collective imagination while most do not. Culture is an evolving, shifting, dynamic phenomenon, and brands ignore this detail at their own peril.

Because of the pitch Suzanne is working on, there's not much time for fun, but after following her and her fabulous boots around for a week and a half, she finds a little time so we can head out to dinner together. We scurry through the rain and into a Soho restaurant.

Once the wine is on the table, it's the perfect time for me to ask, "What's the best example of leading culture you've seen out of the agency?"

"I'd say Domino's," Suzanne says, "because of the long-standing relationship and the measures proving that culture really has shifted for the brand."

When the two companies joined forces back in 2009, Domino's had been in business for fifty years. The problem the brand faced was quickly apparent: The pizza wasn't very good. In fact, on taste it ranked lower than Chuck E. Cheese's, a kids' pizza joint known more for arcade games than food. In focus groups, customers would criticize the food, saying the sauce was like ketchup and the crust was like cardboard.

Suzanne takes a sip of her wine and tells me how the Domino's employees would actually get emotional when they saw focus group footage of people talking about the pizza.

This ignited a push to improve the pizza at Domino's, and CP+B was asked to launch a campaign introducing a new recipe. In response, CP+B asked Domino's to go a step further: They challenged the management team to first apologize for the old product in order to highlight the new one.

To Domino's credit, they completely scrapped their old recipe and developed a product that rated well with people and was still super convenient. Then, taking CP+B's recommendation on board, the advertising showed focus-group footage with real people complaining about the food. Domino's employees would then turn up at the participants' homes (the very people who had complained about the pizza) with the new pizza in hand. They apologized for the old recipe and waited expectantly for each person to taste the new slices. And, of course, the participants loved the new product.

The company was healthy when the new product and campaign hit the market in 2010, but "The Pizza Turn-Around" campaign put a shot of adrenaline into sales, which helped double the share price from $8 to $15 in a year.

Shifting culture can start from a place that's not always pleasant to go: the most uncomfortable truth about a brand or product.

"We've come to call this truth 'the elephant,'" Suzanne says, "playing off the phrase 'elephant in the room.' The elephant is the thing about your brand that creates tension with current culture. If you don't address the elephant, it will continue to create tension and stand in the way, but if you embrace the elephant, it can't be ignored and can lead to wildly successful results."

"The elephant" also works well with Alex Bogusky's fascination with P.T. Barnum. There's a stuffed pygmy elephant named Hermie from Barnum's circus in the Boulder office. It serves as a mascot and inspired the CP+B company logo.

However, in the case of Domino's, addressing their particular elephant (shoddy pizza) could only last for so long. After a while, people started to get bored with the idea. *All right, we get it: You sucked and you fixed it. Let's move on.*

"This led to a lot of work and discussion about where to take the brand next," Suzanne says. "What cultural tension made the most sense to tackle next?"

The full gamut of research, exploration, and analysis ensued. And what came to light this time was the convergence of new inputs: First, one of the most prominent conventions in the pizza category was and still is to shill the deal — the "two pizzas for only $12.99" sort of thing. Second, nearly every franchise owner today started out as a delivery driver. They started from the bottom and now they're here, so to speak. They were living the original American Dream. Third, this was interesting given the post-recession cultural context: People were starting businesses in droves because job security was no more. With the dot-com bust a distant memory, start-up fever had begun to heat up again, and small-business success stories were becoming the new American Dream. The last piece of the puzzle? What food do you order when you're working with a team trying to build a business? Oh yeah, pizza!

The "Powered by Pizza" campaign captured an ideology that elevated the humble slice of pizza to a position of fuel for entrepreneurs. One of the best lines from the anthem spot heard the voice-over declare, "No one's coming up with a world-changing idea with the help of halibut." The idea went beyond ads when Domino's created grants for start-ups called pizzavestments. The phrase "powered by pizza" took off as a hashtag and turned up as a T-shirt design when people ran with the idea themselves.

"I came to CP+B because I had an audacious desire to change things. To imagine that things can be done differently," Suzanne told me. "The Domino's campaign really proves what's possible. Outrageous results come from cultural leadership and challenging conventions."

Domino's is an example of a modern brand that positioned itself to benefit from an emerging culture. And the proof is in the results: Domino's stock price went intergalactic, from $15 to over $100 at the time of writing.

THE ELEPHANT IN THIS BOOK

There's a meta-tension with my entire project that I feel I have to address. Why is it that Suzanne is the only woman who agreed to participate?

I think the answer is layered and nuanced. At the micro level, no woman volunteered. I didn't really know Simon, rOobin, Phil, or Kevin (Chapter 7), but they were bold enough to offer to host me. Beyond these, a few other men offered, but I wasn't able to follow through. I asked many women to participate in hopes of a more equal representation, but I was turned down. The reasons they gave included that they were too busy, too private, or because they worked as freelancers and couldn't imagine a successful two weeks. A few men had this reaction too, but three times as many women made this argument.

Granted, this is not a large-scale sample, but doesn't it indicate something about gender difference? Are women more humble? Less open? Or even afraid that what they say and think is not important? Am I softening my assertions by masking them in questions?

I'll come out and say it then: I don't think many women think they're worth writing about.

I also blame what I'll call "the crumb theory." Imagine you're at home right now and you walk barefoot across your floors. Do you feel crumbs on your feet? I believe women know these sorts of things and are bothered by them more than men. They would feel my eyes noticing and judging their homemaking abilities in a way that most men never think about. So the idea of having another woman in the house and being critically observed is tantamount to torture.

While we do seem to be approaching gender equality in the home, studies show that women still take on more of the responsibilities there. The food preparation, the cleaning, the child care. And it's harder getting ready each day as a woman. I've witnessed the morning routines of a few men now, and these observations are making a strong case for short hair, no makeup, and simpler outfits. It's possible the women I asked are simply too tired to take on one more responsibility, even for two weeks.

Then there's the macro level: I think the odds are bad. There are fewer women in senior positions and, therefore, fewer possible people to make up my sample. Don't misunderstand: I think most levels hire quite equally, but I believe that at the most senior level there's a dearth of female leaders because of a systemic bias. People who are getting their way—in this case, men with fat salaries, autonomy, and substantial egos—don't have any real investment in giving away their power to an "other." Very few women have made it through this gauntlet to demonstrate that there's a place for us younger double X's.

The US government's tallies show that official reports of sexual harassment are in decline, but at the same time, new studies reveal double standards do exist. Rutgers psychology professor Laurie Rudman has conducted a number of experiments in which participants interviewed prospective partners for a competitive game. These experiments suggest that while women who promote themselves and their skills openly are viewed as more competent, they're also viewed as less socially attractive and hirable.

There's also gender bias in interaction. Men may enjoy collaborating with women, but I think this may be outweighed by the trouble opposite sexes have resolving conflict. Being the divorced lady that I am, I've read a lot of armchair psychology on the topic of relationships and discovered the work of marriage researchers Robert W. Levenson and John Gottman. By studying how couples, both straight and gay, interact, the researchers were able to determine which patterns of relating were attributable to gender. What did they discover? Same-sex couples have fewer verbal attacks and make more of an effort to defuse confrontation. They appear to fight more fairly and get over fights more quickly. They are even less likely to experience physical reactions, such as an elevated heart rate and adrenaline surges. If it's so much easier to get along with your own gender, might that raise a pretty high bar for women to get onto the executive committee?

Then there are the career path norms. In most countries, there's not a whole lot of flexibility for women in the years when their children are small. Think about it: When a woman has children, most likely in her thirties, she's just coming into her own in her career. In most advertising jobs, everyone is expected to travel and work late nights, an impossible expectation for parents of young children. There's no "lite" option at work so men or women can step down a couple of rungs on the ladder back to a mid-level role.

Advertising is not a business that encourages alternative paths. The most acceptable path for a woman is to come back from maternity leave and make the best of it. I've known some mothers who switched to HR roles and others who become freelance consultants, but they essentially had to take their ball and go home. Agencies are not in the business of constructing jobs suitable for parents.

There are organizations and events like Lean In and The 3% Conference (the name of which changes each year to match the percentage of women in our industry and is designed to get an increase in that statistic) that have come into being to rally women and supportive men. Sadly, I find the rhetoric to be repetitive: Women are good for business, so if you value the bottom line you'll achieve gender equality. And generally these organizations create an echo chamber among women who are fully engaged and ambitious.

Is my criticism of the advertising industry entirely fair and modern and feminist-approved? No. But then again, life is not fair or modern or feminist-approved. As a result, Suzanne is the sole representative of my own gender in my learning journey.

Despite the industry's unfair gender imbalance, I will say that in doing this project, being female was an advantage for me. I don't think I would have been welcomed into so many homes, full of so many children, if I were a man. So Malcolm Gladwell is right when he states in his book *David and Goliath* that the underdog, if he or she doesn't play to conventions, has the advantage.

Joining forces with Suzanne was like boarding a two-week-long carnival ride: She's always on the move and loads of fun. She's also unlike a two-week-long carnival ride in that I didn't throw up. Not even once. What I came to understand from this jaunt is that we have the power to change culture in the service of brands. If it were easier to do, we'd all get God complexes. Fortunately, it's not so hard as to be impossible.

But it's not merely brands that benefit from leading culture. As an individual, and for me as a woman in business, I can be a part of leading a change in this culture too.

At the end of this whirlwind two weeks in London, Suzanne kindly reminds me, "You're in this to shift the culture of business, Heather. Being female is just one tiny way you're different. What's really going to set you apart is your broad experience, across brands, across companies, across countries and cultures. Hang on to that. It will serve you well."

TENSION

BY SUZANNE POWERS

As it was told to me, the concept of tension was a joint product of Alex Bogusky and Russ Klein, the head client at Burger King at the time. Russ's contribution stemmed from the Freudian thinking that all people are driven by a need to release tension and anxiety. This drive to reduce tension is behind all of our behaviors. So if you could identify a tension people experience *that relates to the brief at hand*, any brand, product or communication that stuck its finger into such a tension would cause people to sit up and take notice. It would go against the grain of cultural norms, so, of course, it would stand out. And if done in a clever enough way, there would be a release—some sort of thought provocation or more often humor—that would earn favor for a brand and, even better, turn people into media who want to spread your idea.

Dr. Stephen Sands, who has studied the brain's response to advertising further bolsters this thinking: "People tend to categorize everything to keep complexity down. The brain would rather not think about things. It's predisposed to toss things away." Therefore, finding relevant tensions helps create work that cannot be ignored.

CP+B's campaign for Baby Carrots is a good example. When we conducted research and went into people's homes to talk about snacks, it quickly became clear that if there were a heat map of the average kitchen, the place where the Doritos live would be red-hot while the crisper is where food goes to die. Carrots can be a snack, but they are also a punishment. Instead of touting vitamin C or a feel-good healthy lifestyle, CP+B took this tension head-on by putting the carrots in junk-food packaging and selling them in vending machines. The work treated baby carrots as though they were just another bad-ass, crunchy, electric-orange snack. The "Eat 'em like junk food" campaign yielded a swirl of press and double-digit sales increases in the two markets where the campaign ran.

Unlike the hundreds of brief formats and brand diagrams I've seen, CP+B has a box labeled "tension." Getting the team to agree to what tension the brand ought to tackle is the subject of much debate. And it's how we are never blindsided by culture. It's not some trend report that's interesting but then forgotten. It's an essential component that aims to shift from current reality toward a new reality in service of the brand.

evolve the
MODEL

KEVIN MAY
Sticks | Seattle

chapter
SEVEN

**"We are happiest when our passions,
our expertise, and our income are fully aligned."**

– Bud Caddell

Maybe I don't belong in an agency—digital, social, or otherwise. The economic crisis of 2008 both instilled fear among clients and introduced dramatic shifts in headcounts at agencies. Really smart, likeable people with good track records started being laid off (or made redundant, depending on geography) in response to increasing client turnover. Security has disappeared, not just in this business, but across the economy. We all understand that we can no longer count on jobs. And we're all supposed to embrace the opportunity to be our own boss, run our own business. Entrepreneurs are becoming the new aspirational elite, their choice cast as an opportunity rather than a free-agent nation necessity.

The entrepreneurial route, with its underlying autonomy, is not without appeal. Would starting my own company provide more satisfaction?

This line of thinking is precisely what brought me to Seattle to work with Kevin May at what he describes as his foundational strategy company, Sticks.

The prospect of two weeks working with Kevin turns my attention toward entrepreneurship. I imagine starting a business requires not only inspiration to craft a fresh business model but also determination to keep learning and evolving in order to grow such a business.

Kevin May, a Brit living in the US, has an eclectic background that includes a degree in theology from Oxford and a disturbing obsession with the Arsenal Football Club. This obsession not only sees him get up at 4:00 a.m. Pacific time to watch their matches kick off, but it also means international flights to a dozen games each year and an inclination to draw on arcane soccer references to casually illustrate points of conversation.

Proving there is life outside of football, Kevin once made a road trip through the forty-eight contiguous United States in forty-eight days, but there was a catch: He set up rules for himself that ensured certain types of interactions. For example, he had to have at least one fifteen-minute conversation with someone who hadn't sold him something, and he had to buy a souvenir from each state, something distinctive enough not to be available in any other state.

I think that whatever in Kevin's character compelled him to make such a trip is probably what also opened him to harboring me on my quest, given I'm obviously never going to become a fellow Arser. Proof of his adventure persists in the form of a Montana turd bird that stares at me from its shelf in the May family's guest room, which doubles as Kevin's den when people aren't staying.

Kevin lives with his wife Christine and their four-year-old daughter Charlotte in a house set on a hill in Seattle's Queen Anne neighborhood, overlooking Puget Sound. To give you one small clue to Kevin's daunting intellect, he's just the sort of bloke who knows the difference between a bay, a sound, a bight, and a fjord. But he's also the sort of guy who proudly displays a framed citation from a brush with the law for public urination outside the Moffat Toffee shop in Scotland back in the 1990s.

When I first Skyped with Kevin, I thought he was just another strategist: intelligent, but fed up with the frustrations of agency life . . . someone who'd now hung out a shingle. Politics was clearly part of his motivation: "I abhor the bullshit of so many agencies," he told me. "Too often they present the illusion of new thinking by just coming up with a new lexicon to describe a bunch of old behaviors, processes, and ways of doing things."

He felt strongly that there had to be a better way to deliver a quality strategic offering, one more fit-for-purpose in the post-digital revolution era, and he had sufficient entrepreneurial spirit to be prepared to fall flat on his face: "I'd rather do something new, even if it means failing spectacularly, than cling to an old mediocrity."

SOMETHING NEW ON THE SOUND

Seattle is a beautiful city where you smell coffee from the moment you land and where you can feel caffeinated electricity in the air. As a rule, the city is mostly cloudy with occasional light drizzle from October to March, so my early December arrival means a cold and gray that is reminiscent of Amsterdam.

After I'd spent a week in Texas with my family for Thanksgiving, Kevin picks me up at Seattle airport on a Monday morning, and we head straight for the office. Nestled in a mostly residential neighborhood, Sticks HQ is no more than a ten-minute walk from the Mays' home. Talk about an easy commute. The street is lined with maples, elms, and plentiful street parking. An interior designer keeps an office next door, and a Trader Joe's market is directly across the street.

The office consists of two meeting rooms—both named after Arsenal references, naturally—with some space for desks in between. Kevin opened for business in 2009 after spending four years leading strategy for Publicis West. Before that, he'd spent twenty-odd years rising through the ranks of various London agencies as an account man turned strategist, finding out along the way that neither door-to-door sales nor journalism was his true calling. The depth and breadth of experiences across adland opened his eyes to several opportunities for doing things differently. On our first day together, he takes me through the origins of the company.

"I made several observations over the years working in agencies," he told me. "First off, unlike other departments, the demand on the strategy group in an agency is much more variable than it is on the other departments. There are periods of time with huge demands on resources, and other periods of just trying to look busy. The department might be the right size for ten weeks of the year, too small for twenty, and too big for the rest.

"Secondly, being in Seattle put me in perpetual recruit mode. There weren't a hundred other agencies in town to poach people from or that would naturally send people my way through churn. I had to constantly be on the lookout, and in so doing I kept finding more and more people who had the word 'strategy' in their title but who did stuff that was completely outside the bounds of my own experience and competency. I loved meeting these people because their interests and expertise meant they looked at things through a completely fresh lens. I really wanted to be able to tap into some of those different perspectives, but at the same time I knew that I'd never be able to offer any of them a full-time post in a static department such as you find in a conventional agency setup."

He also saw huge potential to tap into the freelance workforce. Women especially would leave agencies in droves so they could improve their work/life balance.

"They would become consultants and freelancers simply for the flexibility to pick and choose how much and when they work," Kevin reflected. "And regardless of gender, freelance strategists are not always the best rainmakers. They tend to be more pensive souls who prefer solving problems to generating business, scoping projects, and making deals. They also miss working in teams and miss the access to the sounding boards of other human brains. It can be a lonely life."

But Kevin had also observed a flaw in the agency system: All too often, strategy development is done in a "kick-bollock-scramble" fashion (as Kevin puts it).

"You'd be briefed by a client one day, with the expectation that you'd brief the creative teams no later than the next day," Kevin said. "This gives very limited opportunity for the strategic input to do any of the heavy lifting. The net result is that all that responsibility falls on the shoulders of the creative department, with agencies using creative development as a highly inefficient means of teasing out what the brief should have been in the first place."

Creative teams *are* terribly pressured, but at least it's recognized that what they do requires some time to think. Not so the strategist. Whether it's a brief, POV, or a proposal, "I haven't had a chance to think it through" is generally not an acceptable response. Putting resources against the wrong brief is terribly inefficient, but it seems to be the dominant practice. This only perpetuates an inability for clients to imagine what executions might come out of a brief and a propensity to force-fit multiple problems, observations, and contradictions into briefs.

All of these observations slowly fed Kevin's hunch that some sort of fluid community that encompassed a huge array of expertise, experience, and perspective could be engaged on an as-needed basis to interrogate problems and figure out which ones need solving. The idea was to build something that behaved just like a creative department—with collaboration, thinking time, risk-embracing culture, and high-quality filters—but which produced a strategic output.

"I expected the biggest challenge to be finding the people, so I spent the first three months just having chats with potential participants, clients, and partners. I started with a list of only four contacts that I thought could help me build something, and each person led to additional introductions. There was almost unanimous support for the idea—at least in theory—and in those first few months, I found forty-five people with varying degrees of enthusiasm."

Instead of calling people off the bench *pro re nata* to run projects, Kevin started engaging people for just a day or an afternoon, using a trial-and-error method.

"I began with the goodwill of people to help me get Sticks off the ground by donating their time. To figure out if the model would 'groove,' I drummed up eleven projects that we did for free using a total of twenty-one people from our embryonic roster. We learned quickly, mainly about what *not* to do. I soon realized that we got more done in a two-hour session than if we made people stay for a whole afternoon. We also found the magic number was four people in the room, but at least three and certainly *never* more than five, at which point the forum seems to change fundamentally.

"With those first projects, we landed on some key aspects of Sticks that have abided to this day. Not only are we very careful about length and size of these sessions, we cast for diversity first and specific experience second. We focus on finding new questions rather than rushing to solutions. And we built a toolbox around a philosophy of creating attractiveness for brands rather than just trying to force attention."

Kevin had stumbled upon a commercial revival of the salon, and this structure became the special sauce of Sticks. Today, Kevin will include four or five sessions in the scope of every project. Far from pompous and grandiose as the word "salon" might imply, these sessions have proved to be stimulating and fun for participants while at the same time being a cost-effective and potent tool for the business of strategy.

"Do any clients attend the sessions?" I ask.

"On rare occasions, but generally it's more the sausage being made in the back," he says. "They're more concerned with the output I deliver. But because I get to better solutions by utilizing the sessions, and that so dramatically influences the output, I've learned to put a lot of effort into the type of environment we create, not just what we ask people to do and how we deploy them."

Some of the lessons he's learned in crafting the salons include making the work interesting and fun, and above all creating a place that people like going to. The in-person aspect, as opposed to working with a virtual network, contrasts significantly with the world of crowdsourcing. These are brains physically coming together and getting to experience the joy of stimulation from the other brains.

"I've been able to attract disproportionately talented people to come and work with us because of the environment," he says. "I'd say it's the single thing we've got most consistently right, and it's why we've been able to stay in business when the economic climate of the past few years has so often worked against us."

During my stay with Kevin, I participated in six salon sessions for a variety of projects, from naming a new app-centered business and fine-tuning their position to grappling with what considerations might matter in bringing a US brand into China. Kevin has perfected the formula for creating this mystically magnetic environment: always start and finish on time, pay participants well (and within twenty-four hours), and begin by riffing on the assignment but let the participants take the conversation wherever it may go. At the end of one session I attended, one participant—an ex-CMO from the client side—gushed, "This was the best two hours of my career to date. This is what I always imagined working in marketing would be like when I chose this as a career."

I'm left with the realization that such a setup is simple and easy to implement, so why hasn't anyone in any of the perhaps hundreds of agencies and consultancies I've worked in and visited tried such a thing before?

GENUINE AUTHENTICITY

It's 2:00 p.m., and Kevin has invited two Sticks members, Scott and Keri, to join us for a salon. Teas and coffees are made, and we settle into one of the meeting areas.

Microsoft has asked Kevin to help them think about pirated software in China, and this is the very first foray into the project.

"Hopefully, this is a subject that none of you has ever given much thought to before," Kevin tells us as he closes the door to the room and picks up a dry-erase marker. "Here's how this will work: The next two hours are purposely unstructured. We'll be talking about Microsoft, which has asked us to think about pirated software in China. The situation there is very different from things in the West, where almost all machines come with an operating system installed. In China, the norm is for the machines to come unloaded and for the customer to make a separate purchase for all the software. And while the genuine stuff runs comfortably into three figures, rip-off versions are available for about a dollar in the same stores that sell the machines.

"Microsoft would understandably like to increase preference for authentic products, but that's not our goal today. This is not a new problem for the company, and it's something they've spent tons of effort and money trying to solve. We're not going to come up with the answer straight off the bat, but if we can find just one question this client has never thought to ask about this aspect of their business, that will be a success for this session."

With the ground rules covered and the issue at hand presented, we begin to discuss what authenticity means and why it matters to people. We struggle at first. That a genuine product can reduce the risk of an operating system failure seems unlikely to matter to people who live in a culture accepting of pirating.

What about the real deal product giving the user extra status? Well, we don't exactly "show off" our operating systems, and it's unlikely that a bystander could determine the provenance of your operating system when you're using your computer. It's not like a Louis Vuitton bag or Ray-Ban sunglasses where quality issues might be visible to the eye.

This is a tough one.

We discuss the cultural environment today, where it's socially acceptable to obtain pirated copies of any content. It's as though the copies are not real. It's too easy to make copies, and companies like Microsoft make so much money that no one feels sorry for them.

I bring up the book *The Geography of Thought,* which Jason Oke introduced me to when I visited him in Hong Kong. In the book, Richard Nisbett challenges the outdated assumption that all people have the same basic cognitive processes and use the same rules for reasoning. For example, in Eastern cultures, the collective matters more than the desires of the individual. As members of a collective, could Microsoft come to some sort of culturally amenable, harmonious compromise?

Scott points out that the Microsoft stock price has been flat since Steve Ballmer has taken the reins, and there seems to be a lack of vision for the future. Perhaps some open-source software is inevitable, and Microsoft is not thinking of its role in light of such inevitability.

"Microsoft seemed to miss the inevitability of search as a revenue stream, even though they created the widely used tool Internet Explorer to navigate the Web," Scott says. "What would the implication be to offer the most copied applications for free? If we were to accept free software as an inevitability, how else might we focus the business?"

We discuss the psychology of receiving something for free. People are hardwired to reciprocate when they receive something of value, but the near invisibility of software and the standard acceptance of cheap pirated copies means there is little appreciation of the operating system as something to be grateful for. The reciprocity impulse isn't activated. What would have to happen to activate it? Could the product be designed where the free version locks a person into the channel and a paid version would unlock additional benefits?

Every now and then, Kevin jumps up and jots something on the whiteboard signaling that someone has just said something "really fucking interesting" (as Kevin would put it). Laptops and phones were banished in the salon, but I never had that impulse to check for messages as the two hours flew by.

At the end of the session, the wall is filled, but nobody can remember who said what. It's been an extraordinarily collaborative session, and the notes on the board already show a completely unexpected series of emerging patterns.

There is a striking difference between a salon and a brainstorm: We're not pressing to solve the problem; instead, we're sizing up the problem, picking it up, and examining the texture and weight. We're all bringing in our own experiences and seeing how they fit together. Each person offered relevant input but had completely different ways of viewing the same problem.

I was hooked. We'd managed to create the caliber of conversation that I most love in my work but that only seems to happen when the stars align. It was intellectually stimulating while at the same time being further proof that the salon is a powerful business tool to achieve "multidisciplinary randomness," as another friend and strategist, Faris Yakob, calls it. Differences in how we think—our heuristics, perspectives, interpretations, mental models—that's what improves our collective ability to solve problems.

A different Scott, Scott Page, in his book *The Difference: How the Power of Diversity Creates Better Groups, Firms, Schools, and Societies,* delves into diversity and its impact on tackling tasks. Where some tasks reflect the sum of the individuals, like a relay race, others are disproportionately influenced by the weakest member, where one person can bring the whole group down, like in, say, a musical trio. But then there are the tasks where one person can bring the whole group *up.* These are called disjunctive tasks, and they best define the nature of strategic business problems where diversity enhances ability. "Diversity," Scott Page says, "works best on disjunctive tasks because multiple approaches can be tried simultaneously, and one good idea means success for everybody."

One good idea. We've all held one of those in our hands. They are precious.

After this salon session, I feel as though we're far closer to asking a question that will lead to a good idea than we would be if we'd each spent two weeks pondering the issue on our own.

MAKE IT UP

A month after Steve Jobs died, PBS ran a documentary on his life (*One Last Thing*), which includes one of his most inspiring quotes: "Life can be much broader once you discover one simple fact, and that is, everything around you that you call life was made up by people that were no smarter than you, and you can change it, you can influence it, you can build your own things that other people can use. Once you learn that, you'll never be the same again."

What do I take from this quote? We're limited only by our imaginations.

So why does it seem that there are so few who have learned this lesson and struck out to change things?

I'm inspired by visionaries like a Tony Hsieh, founder of Zappos, who has not only found a way to make customer service so good it's differentiating but has also invested the proceeds from the sale of his company to Amazon into an urban resuscitation of downtown Las Vegas. Pegged as the Downtown Project, his goal is to create a convergence of the TED, SXSW, and Burning Man lifestyles in one place. Ambitious double whammy.

I'm disheartened, though, when I look specifically at the world of business strategy companies. The diffusion curve of innovation theory suggests that 2.5 percent of strategy practitioners should fit into the category of innovators—those actively willing to take risks and who are either coming up with the new ways of working or who have the financial wherewithal to bring the ideas to market. Yet, I am hard-pressed to find many companies that are pushing their models into the fringe of strategy methodologies.

Advertising agencies are always ready to jump on a trend, so it's rare to find one in business today without a lab version of itself. I struggle with counting the agency labs as real risks. Most buy a 3-D printer and trot out interesting ideas, but ultimately they exist more to create cachet rather than revenue, operating on the margins as a defense mechanism instead of permeating the culture and evolving their model.

Other innovations have emerged in the form of virtual collectives like a Victors & Spoils or Ideasicle. They are harnessing the wisdom of crowds. The innovation consultancy Evolution is matching start-ups with large bureaucratic brands to help them innovate, and, a bit farther afield, the digitally savvy consultancy Undercurrent is implementing a new organizational structure called holocracy— the anti-hierarchy. No search could be fully exhaustive, but mine left me feeling that the percentage of entrepreneurs trying new methodologies is much less than 2.5 percent.

Even the list of failures is rather slim. Do you recall Agency Nil? They purported to offer branding and advertising services that were crowdsourced from their network, and clients would then pay what they thought the ideas were worth. But then they simply disappeared, and quickly. Collectively, new models—both those still in business and the failures—represent a small slice of the number of people taking risks to start something from scratch. That's why I think what Kevin is doing is actually profound.

I must admit, I've had a bunch of ideas over the years for service businesses. For example, living in Amsterdam and meeting a real dominatrix with a dungeon made me wonder if I could start a company called "Shut Up and Take It" where clients would agree to submit to whatever the company recommends. I once read that many people in retirement communities receive no visitors, and it made me wonder if there might be a mutually beneficial partnership with the elderly. Tapping into all of that life experience could be a very interesting way to solve business problems. (Turns out IDEO had a similar notion and recently hired a ninety-year-old designer who works in the Silicon Valley office one day a week). On another occasion, watching the documentary *Neurons to Nirvana* while living in Amsterdam sparked an idea to harness the power of drugs to shake loose transformational business ideas for clients. Unfortunately, nothing has come to mind that I thought I must seriously pursue.

After work on Thursday evening, Kevin and I head to a restaurant just around the corner from the office. It's called, strikingly, How to Cook a Wolf. We munch on polenta fritters and talk about what it is about him that got him to leap.

"I'd sit in these agency management meetings, discussing our own agency positioning," Kevin says. "I'd ask, 'What do we believe in?' and I'd be met with blank stares. The best work and commercial success seems to come from those companies that stand for something more than just doing what's necessary to still be in business next week. We'd preach such thinking to our clients all the time, so I'd go on and say, 'Well, all right, what *won't* we do? Even if our most profitable client called up and demanded it, what's on the list of things we'd refuse? Let me start. I'll throw out murder. Any advice on that for where we'd draw the line?'

"I assumed, rightly, that we wouldn't do contract killings, even if a client threatened to take their business away. But when this was met with further blank stares, I made the observation that 'The agency that refuses to do murders' is not much of a positioning.

"Advertising execution has become increasingly commoditized. We all get that the world has moved on from the thirty-second TV commercial, so beyond embracing some new paradigm, ad agencies are rushing to find the 'thing' that makes them appear differentiated. But none of the ones I've worked with was willing to try anything more substantial than renaming 'big idea' to 'contagious idea' and then just carry on doing the same stuff."

"All companies need a 'thing,' right?" I say. "Otherwise you're simply trading on the reputation of the founder."

"If I knew only one thing when I started," Kevin says, "I knew for certain that the name of the business wasn't going to have anything to do with my name. Not only does it make it harder to feel like a company when you do that, it was never going to be about me as fount, only as catalyst. Our clients come back to us because of the quality of our collective output, and because we don't behave like we have the answer to every problem. And I also wanted to avoid that convention from the agency world to name the place after the founders, who often turn out to be egomaniacal tossers."

I think that's why there are many firms named after the founder that stay around the twenty-person size. The founder is expected in every meeting, which limits the number of clients they can take on. The inherent expectation of having the founder involved in everything hinders growth, because a founder's time is not scalable.

The other benefit of not naming the company after himself seems to be the ability to separate himself from it enough to take breaks. As the founder of a young company, Kevin makes the effort to have a life outside of work (and this sometimes extends to something non-Arsenal related). For example, the Mays had already planned to head up to Vancouver for the weekend in the midst of my visit and invited me to tag along. The Vancouver fire department puts together an amazing annual Christmas light extravaganza where you ride on a small train through the city park to view different themed displays. Charlotte's favorite included a Rudolph wearing a white leisure suit dancing to Village People's "YMCA" on twelve-foot stilts. Even in the business of Christmas, there's an opportunity to innovate.

A STRIKE OF THE EYE

Each morning at the Mays' house, Kevin gets up first to make tea for the adults and warm milk for Charlotte. It was a thoughtful surprise for me to open the guest room door and find a hot cuppa there the first morning. We sit at their breakfast table one morning, finishing our tea and chatting. Their windows look out over the water, and the Olympic Mountains come into view on the horizon as the fog recedes. We've discussed strategy for more than a week now, but it just struck me that Kevin, through Sticks, has harnessed a belief about how strategy works that I'd also read about in *Strategic Intuition,* a book by William Duggan.

In his book, Columbia Business School professor Duggan investigates the discipline of military strategy and its foundational role in current business strategy. He presents two separate historians who attempted to codify Napoleon's military success and arrived at two very different conclusions. First is Baron Antoine Jomini, who spent ten years in the French army and suggested that Napoleon's success was the outcome of strategic planning. He outlined a three-step process for military strategy that begins with determining where you are (Point A), deciding where you want to go (Point B), and then devising a plan to get from Point A to Point B.

When I read about this in Duggan's book, I realized Stephen King, one of the founders of strategy in the advertising agency, had imported this process at J. Walter Thompson (JWT). He built on the three steps, adding a reflection on why we are where we are now and taking stock of how the plan worked before entering the cycle again.

Contrast Jomini's strategic planning with Carl von Clausewitz's *coup d'oeil*, a visceral French term meaning "strike of the eye," to describe what Duggan renamed *strategic intuition*. Clausewitz was an opponent of Napoleon in the Prussian army, and he outlined his own four-stage process for military strategy. First, you pull information from history (your own applicable experiences and whatever you can learn), and then you clear your mind of specific objectives or preordained solutions. Next, you synthesize relevant thoughts into a new way forward (the flash of insight in the mind that strikes the eye), and finally end with the resolve and determination to carry out the new idea.

Duggan suggests that, beyond its difficult-to-pronounce name, Clausewitz's theory of *coup d'oeil* (published in his book *On War*) remained obscure for two reasons. First, it was written in dense, academic German, whereas Jomini wrote in clear, easy-to-understand French. Second, given the book was published in 1832, there was no understanding of neuroscience or of just how ideas form in the brain. We now know that ideas happen when several regions of the brain fire at once. A workable combination of previously unconnected elements is the fundamental definition of an idea.

That strategic development has so thoroughly dominated the business world is yet another reason for the current success of Sticks, a company designed for strategic intuition.

"Given strategy development is such an unruly mental process," I say to Kevin, "do lots of people end up having ideas in the shower or while driving rather than in the salon?"

Kevin collects Charlotte's backpack from the kitchen table and wrangles her into her coat. "Well, a crucial part of our deal with participants is how self-contained the salons are: We require no prep and no follow-up, just an engaged brain for the time that they are with us. That said, we very often do receive a whole load of subsequent rumination from some people. I think that's due largely to how we engage with them. They are much more inclined to want to reciprocate with overdelivery. We also anticipate percolation in that we never do anything with the whiteboard of a salon for at least twenty-four hours, usually more than forty-eight hours, after it's finished. Then we return to it and see what has trickled down in our own consciousnesses, and we make sure that the stuff we thought was brilliant a couple of days beforehand still feels like that."

THE P WORD

The Point-A-to-Point-B way of thinking about strategy development seduced me early on in my career by its sheer simplicity, but upon reflection, and especially after participating in Sticks' method of diverse perspectives coming together in a salon, the "strike of the eye" strategic intuition seems a far more accurate description of what I myself have experienced in strategy work. As I've evolved and gained more knowledge, it has become easier to come up with ideas for brands at the intersection of rigorous data collection and lateral thinking. But I wouldn't call generating strategic options "planning" per se. I feel using the words "plan" and "planning" creates an unwarranted focus on the outcome, the plan, and misdirects attention from the more important process of strategic intuition.

Tacitly, I think the rest of the strategy community is coming to the same conclusion. Let's go back in time for a moment: In the world of advertising, a "voice of the consumer" discipline originated in the late sixties when Stanley Pollitt (at Boase Massimi Pollitt) and Stephen King (at JWT) concurrently introduced account planners to the agency. It was Tony Stead at JWT who named the discipline "account planning" at a company off-site.

Planners were charged with being nosy. They were the ones learning about people, brands, categories, and culture and bringing the relevant pieces forward through a strike of the eye to create effective advertising. The word "plan" focuses on the output of intentional actions, but the emphasis of this job has always been about coming up with rigorously grounded ideas for brands.

The rest of the world has been less attached to the misnomer of "planner," instead morphing their preferred titles to "brand strategist" or just "strategist." While the job was once confined mostly to ad-campaign development, today it has proliferated into all aspects of marketing and exists in-house within the brands and outside among consultancies and agencies of all types. The clan of people who do this work find themselves creating competitive advantages anywhere they can, across all touch points, and even changing existing products and developing new ones.

If the fact that strategists aren't simply making plans isn't reason enough to drop the word "planner," the cult fascination with start-ups tips the balance in favor of letting it go. Academics have analyzed modes of thinking that entrepreneurs employ and found that they operate differently than most corporate execs. Rather than trying to predict what will happen by thinking about it, plotting and sticking to a rigid plan, entrepreneurs act on what they know at the time, learn from their action, then build on what they've created.

Leonard Schlesinger, Charles Kiefer, and Paul Brown are three such academics who differentiate these modes of thinking in their book, *Just Start*. They've named the start-up way of thinking "creaction," a clunky portmanteau meant to articulate creating through action.

They argue that when working within a highly predictable environment or situation, we *should* use predictive thinking and plan; but when we're operating in an uncertain world, the only chance we have to possibly control an unpredictable future is to create it. Or creact it.

Blech. I know we humans are rarely comfortable with the new so I continue to roll this word off the tongue, but that still hasn't made it any more appealing, so I'm not recommending anyone change their title to "creactionist."

Instead, I'm sticking with "strategist," because what we do has proved most useful for businesses operating in a more complex, uncertain time—even more so, I believe, than it did in a more simplistic, predictive one. Grant McCracken's *Culturematic*, which I mentioned in Chapter 1, or Peter Sims's *Little Bets*, are both chock-full of examples of creaction in action. It takes a strategic mind performing strategic intuition to come up with ideas that could prove successful in an unpredictable environment.

On a sunny Thursday morning, Kevin takes me for coffee at Café Fonté, near the famous Pike's Place market. Of course, they roast their own coffee, but the minimalist décor is more Scandi than grunge. It's the perfect setting to bring up the topic of planner versus strategist with Kevin.

"You must have noticed," I begin, "that someone will have the title 'planner' today and 'strategist' tomorrow. There's no distinction in my mind between the two titles that would help me categorize people."

"To me, there's only a historical distinction," Kevin says. "Before the Internet, the planner handled consumer research and wrote propositions. That job doesn't exist anymore. We all have to have a broader purview. And I think that's leading to frustration in advertising. You're learning to think broadly, which is necessary to think about communication today, but, paradoxically, you're also being kept in a box that focuses only on affecting communication in very narrow ways: basically, the ways that allow the agency to make money out of the situation."

"That makes me think of one of the things that's surprised me in the survey over the years," I say. "The average head of planning/strategy has ten years of experience in the discipline, and they've been working for seventeen years. That's not a whole career. It's not the capstone job I thought it was when I started out. Sure, some people make it their life's work, but I think a lot of people I've talked to take their skills and move on to something broader."

"And you're right there in terms of your work experience," Kevin says, polishing off his coffee. "It's really not surprising that you wanted to take on this project now. It'll be interesting to see where you land."

THE ODD-LOOKING GINGER WHO GETS THE GIRLS

Caring about the distinction between planner and strategist could be construed as navel-gazing. What does it really matter if we're all doing the same work? Well, I think the details matter. I think communicating clearly matters. If we can't express what it is we do, how can we hope to do so for brands?

As my trip to Seattle reaches a close, there's a last detail that I find Kevin has zeroed in on to steer the work he does, and it's one I want to discuss with him: creating attractive brands as opposed to generating attention for brands.

On my last night, as Christine puts Charlotte to bed, Kevin and I dig into Thai takeout at the kitchen table, and he tells me a story that influenced how he thinks about brands:

"I had a good mate in London, a northern bloke called Deano, who was a total machine when it came to getting girls. You'd never have expected it from his appearance. He was gawky-looking with ginger hair, and quite some distance from what you'd call classically handsome. But he had two qualities that most blokes fail dramatically at. The first was being just hugely attentive. He made any woman he was talking to feel like they were the complete focus of his attention. His gaze never darted around the room, or even down at their tits. Instead, he kept it fixed right on their eyes. The second was that he was utterly resilient. Even if he got blown off with the most humiliating put-down, he'd just shrug his shoulders, laugh, and carry on with his evening. Within a couple of minutes, he'd be talking to another beauty, completely unabashed by his recent scrape. There was not a scintilla of desperation about him."

"Scintilla, really?" I say. "OK, keep going."

"Well, the age of interruption has passed," Kevin says, "and people are no longer grateful for the chance to buy any company's products or services. Customers today have a surfeit of information and choice. Brands must come to terms with this, similar to the way Deano did. Men generally have a fairly limited artillery when it comes to trying to impress women: Some are good-looking, some are funny, some are clever, some are powerful. Pretty much the same can be said of the traditional approach brands use to market themselves. But Deano figured out that he could gain a significant edge by not only paying attention but also making clear that he was doing so. It proved a ridiculously successful strategy. If all he'd had was his swagger, then I suspect his strike rate would have been significantly more modest, but an equally important factor in his success was not being totally in thrall to his audience. Brands also need that resilience, or they end up standing for nothing.

"What we've done with Sticks is think of a brand in terms of its essential attractiveness. It's not enough to just be a funny, confident, or good-looking brand. You have to understand how you're useful, what makes you likeable, and what makes people want to identify with you." (See *Essential Attractiveness*)

As of this writing, Sticks has done over 250 jobs, and all but three clients have provided return business. When I ask Kevin whether he considers the business a success, he pauses before launching into a review.

"The most important 'success' for me is to have built a financially viable business that has totally eliminated any 'arseholes' from our purview," he says. "We don't have any of them, either as colleagues or as clients, and this is the first time in my career I've been able to say that. We also do work that I'm consistently proud of; if I had to list the best ten things I've ever been associated with in my working life, probably eight of them have happened since I started Sticks.

"My learning curve is steeper than it's been for some years, not only because we're breaching new terrain but because I'm constantly surrounded by people who look at things through completely fresh lenses. And, while it took twenty-one months before I made any income personally from the business—and another year after that until I was back up to where I'd been at my last agency job—we've consistently paid our people well and on time since the end of that initial period of pro bono projects. To date, that figure runs comfortably into seven figures, and, while it may not be particularly rich beer compared to most ad agencies, it's still income people have taken home to their families that just wouldn't otherwise have existed. So I guess those are the things that please me most about these first few years of Sticks."

I'm wooed by Kevin's way of looking at brands, evolving a consultative model in his business and setting his own definition of success. I'm truly inspired to mull over my own entrepreneurial impulses.

ESSENTIAL ATTRACTIVENESS
the guiding principle of sticks

BY KEVIN MAY

The Sticks approach puts Attractiveness at the center of brand strategy because we believe this is more fit-for-purpose in the post-digital world than models based on impact and interruption. There are three component layers that ladder up to this Essential Attractiveness: Utility, Aesthetic, and Values.

Utility encompasses all the areas in which the brand is useful to the people we want to be attracted to us. These are not just the functional benefits but anything tangible about the whole experience of the brand. This could include the physical properties of the product but also things like its pricing, its distribution, and its delivery mechanism. It covers anything that can be objectively assessed concerning a customer and a brand.

Aesthetic encompasses anything that makes the brand likeable to the people we want to be attracted to us. These are not just matters of design, but anything that can be felt or perceived (however intangibly) by those who come into contact with the brand. While it could include traditional brand assets like advertising, taglines and logos, it's also about the personality of the brand, and its overall tone and manner. It covers anything that can be subjectively assessed about being a customer of the brand.

Values encompasses all the things that make the people we want to be attracted to us identify with the brand. These are the things that make them say/think, "People like me have this brand in their lives." This includes the things for which the brand stands, the company it keeps, and the activity it engages in that goes beyond its core transactional business. It's the stuff that strikes at why the brand exists and what it really believes in, and, while mission statements can help point to this, it's much more about how the brand walks the walk (rather than just talks the talk).

LIVE
in the
FUTURE

SAHER SIDHOM

AMV BBDO/Forge Future Factory | London

chapter

EIGHT

**"The future belongs to the few of us
still willing to get our hands dirty."**

– Roland Tianco

"You turn it on; it makes a sound." Saher's voice is gentle and hypnotic, accented with the hint of a native Arabic speaker. "You place your hand above the sensor, like this, and as you move closer or farther away, the pitch changes. Simple."

Saher Sidhom is building an Arduino prototype and showing me how it works. The small device whines like the eerie sound track to the 1950s' version of *The Day the Earth Stood Still.*

I've heard about Arduinos before, read a few articles here and there, but there had been no magnetic appeal that sent me racing to the store to buy one of these little open-source electronic circuit boards. But now that I'm getting the chance to play with one and see how such simple technology can create a tangible branded experience, I'm starting to understand how prototyping is critical.

I've come to Forge, the Future Factory, which is part of AMV BBDO (AMV), one of London's most awarded and respected advertising agencies, to try my hand at making ideas more real—especially ideas that use disruptive technologies.

Of late, many agencies have started initiatives that involve adding "lab" to their name. Sometimes these initiatives look like a last-ditch effort to keep a creative director partner interested, and sometimes they smell of trying desperately not to look as old school and staid as the agency's lobby and letterhead. Knowing Forge is part of one of London's oldest advertising agencies, I'm a little cynical and curious to see what Forge is all about.

There's evidence that AMV is on the right track. They've had great success with clients such as Wrigley's brand "5," which is a gum designed to stimulate the senses. AMV and Wrigley collaborated with a video-game company to develop *The Nightjar*, a "video game with no video." Benedict Cumberbatch's bewitching voice-over guides you as you find yourself stranded on the Nightjar spaceship as it tumbles toward a black hole. You have only your sense of hearing to help you work your way out of this pickle. The game has won dozens of awards and is a great example of branded content worth paying for: The mobile app pulls in $3.99 per download.

Further evidence in AMV's favor is their investment in Saher and his team of three who make up Forge. Saher added "Future Factory" to the name because a factory implies making. "Intellectualism is good to get an understanding of the context," he told me when I brought up the idea of coaching me, "but with technology, you have to think with your hands because you learn by doing. The insight is in the making."

Thirty-nine-year-old Saher is Sudanese and Egyptian by background but grew up in London as the youngest of three brothers. He also lived in Sweden for a number of years. He has several distinguishing peculiarities: He wears only black on weekdays and only gray on weekends, with yellow as an accent since—in addition to being a sunny and optimistic color—it's the color of creativity. No matter the color, his style leans to what he calls "combat tech." He shaves his head, wears designer clear-rimmed glasses, and is a head or so shorter than me. Like many successful entrepreneurs, he left university early and founded a start-up. The company's business model was based on a daily deal idea, similar to Groupon. It was ahead of its time—this was in the nineties—but it gave him a baptism by fire into entrepreneurism. Since then, he's worked for a number of well-respected companies including AKQA, Great Works, and Ogilvy, and he's taught for Berghs School of Communication, IBIS, Google Squared, and Hyper Island.

These school connections have proven useful, because Saher has gathered a group of twenty bright people—half of them students, the other half early-in-their-career technologists—for a hack week. He invited me to observe and participate with this diverse group who hail from twelve nations and will tackle live briefs. These designers and developers were chosen, like the attendees of Kevin May's salons, for their diversity of perspectives: The rooms will be packed with programmers, artists and strategists, each lending their unique skills.

Oh, plus a drone. You can't have a hackathon without a drone.

THE TECHNOLOGY RADAR

On my first evening in his home, Saher prepares a risotto while I snoop around his open kitchen, dining room, and living room, drinking wine and chatting with him as he stirs.

Saher lives alone, but his flat lacks any telltale signs of a bachelor. Shoes come off at the front door. Fresh daffodils sit in a vase on the table. They're yellow, and so too are the teakettle, toaster, coffeemaker, hourglass, and oversized decorative LEGO man head. The uncluttered space is punctuated with tasteful décor, like his collection of vintage cameras and a painting with "Unique Master" written in Chinese characters. And did I mention he knows how to make a mushroom, sun-dried-tomato, white-wine risotto?

"I want my home to be serene," he tells me as I move from item to item. "A place where I can recollect my thoughts."

One wall of the living room faces the Thames, and through the floor-to-ceiling windows I can see boats moored below, bobbing in the cold water. Just to the right, the majestic Tower Bridge stands illuminated. Not a bad view at all.

A small remote-controlled gadget sits next to the television. It's a plastic 3-D word, "FUCK," in all-caps with rotor blades attached. Technically, it's a flying fuck.

I make my way back to the open kitchen and lean against the counter, watching the maestro at work. "Other than the flying fuck, you're not especially gadget-y," I say. "Were you the type of kid that took the radio apart?"

Saher smiles as he adds broth to the pan. "Well, I wasn't a romantic tinkerer like that, but I grew up with two older brothers who were engineers. The oldest was an electrical engineer who was constantly building things with electronics—you know, making things that lit up or made sounds, that sort of thing. The other was a civil engineer with lots of cool architectural tools and a special desk. So sketching and making were just daily activities in our household when I was a child.

"I remember one time I designed this early warning system where a light would come on in our flat when someone stepped on the bottom step of the staircase."

"That's pretty neat!" I say. "I think the techiest thing I made as a kid wasn't until high school. I programmed a little animated astronaut jumping across the moon using Pascal." I shrug, and Saher smiles again and nods knowingly.

"With programming, once the Internet came round, it was natural to start building Web things," Saher says. "A mate of mine who wanted to start an online shopping business in those early days told me what he had in mind, and I built him a prototype site that did about 80 percent of what he wanted. I just started making something the day he told me the idea, and I stayed up all night playing with it. He was astonished and took it into a pitch a week later and landed one million in VC."

"You had to crush my astronaut, didn't you?" I say, duly impressed.

Saher laughs and plates up our supper. "I didn't always know what I was doing. I would just tinker, break, build."

Given that creativity is a combination of two things that haven't been combined before, you have to know the technology if you want to create something with it. In his book *Paid Attention,* Faris Yakob calls technology a medium, a unique one that "provides a canvas that is yet to be effectively colonized by the amateur," as opposed to text, images, and video that the masses can now easily play with.

I love this idea of technology as a medium. Durex's Fundawear springs to mind: electronic underwear where your partner, with the help of a handy app, can send vibrations through your knickers when you're near or far. Fundawear communicates Durex's fun-filled attitude toward sex in a way a TV spot or coupon just can't. It cuts through precisely because it's not easy for just anyone to make their own Fundawear (at least, not without ending up in the hospital). For Durex, or any brand, the challenge is having enough familiarity with technology to push past what an amateur would create.

At the table, I ask Saher how he keeps up with new technology.

"Personally, I watch a lot of documentaries. There are a few great books like *Physics of the Future* and *Superintelligence* that I'd recommend, but really you can't help but read about tech every day. You've shown me five things I didn't know about since you got here. We're inundated with it. The trick is, I think, not letting it just pass by as a fleeting blip on the radar. 'Radar' is the perfect word actually. Do you know about Gartner's Technology Hype Cycle?"

"I know Gartner, but not about the Hype Cycle," I say.

"It's a chart they put together each year that places emerging technologies across a spectrum from the initial breakthrough to mass adoption. In the early days, when something is first invented, people have insanely high expectations to the point of disillusionment of what that technology will do for society. But as time goes by, we figure out just how we can and can't use a technology. We have to be aware of as many technologies as possible, but also keep track of how they evolve over time." (See *Collaborative Innovation*)

Later, when I have time to ponder what Saher has said, it sinks in that our job as marketers is not just to see things coming but to keep them in our sights as they morph and develop. Some things, like the LED screen known as Disco Dog, which can turn your pet into a moving mini-billboard, are gimmicks and probably won't cut through for long. Other things, like the smartphone, will continue to rock our world as, one by one, every device we ever loved in the eighties and nineties finds itself replaced by apps inside the phone.

Hyper Island has a workshop tool called Future Mapping, which is designed to help a group co-create a physical radar of sorts (see toolbox.hyperisland.com). The group is prompted to remember as many technologies as they can that came down the pipe in recent memory, like, say, Bluetooth. Each technology goes on a Post-it on a timeline. Then the group is asked to populate the near future with things that aren't yet mainstream but we know are possible, like self-driving cars, delivery by drone, and petri-dish-produced protein. Last, the group stretches further and predicts what might be possible five to ten years from the present.

Doing this exercise raises the collective team knowledge of technologies, which makes the relevant ones top of mind for present and future projects—and doing it every quarter or every month institutionalizes the importance of such knowledge in innovating. A timeline like this, prominently displayed and frequently updated, reminds me of a highly alert air traffic controller monitoring the sweeping line passing over his radar display screen again and again. It takes consistent attention to do the job right.

THE ART OF THE HACK

After I've spent a couple of days settling into Saher's routine, Wednesday arrives, and so too do the hackers for the hackathon. While the word "hack" might first conjure images of unathletic individuals hunched over laptops, typing their way into databases where they don't belong, the meaning here is quite different. Programmers use the word "hack" to mean an ingenious solution to a problem. Add "-athon," and you've got an event designed to reach ingenious solutions in a preset amount of time.

At its essence, a hackathon speeds up the exploration of "the adjacent possible," as Steven Johnson describes it in his book *Where Good Ideas Come From*:

> *Think of [the adjacent possible] as a house that magically expands with each door you open. You begin in a room with four doors, each leading to a new room that you haven't visited yet. Once you open one of those doors and stroll into that room, three new doors appear, each leading to a brand-new room that you couldn't have reached from your original starting point. Keep opening new doors and eventually you'll have built a palace.*

This beautiful metaphor captures the act of creativity itself. Previously unconnected thoughts combine into new ideas that press human potential ever forward. At any given time, in any given discipline, new ideas are hovering, waiting at the edge of the yet-to-be-expanded palace, ready for us to open the next door.

Forge has a dedicated space on the ground floor of AMV BBDO. There are four sizeable offices for teams to work in, each with actual doors to close, a rare luxury in most advertising agencies these days. When London weather cooperates, there's even access to daylight through exterior windows. Each office has a glass wall facing an open central staging area, which is where Saher gathers the entire group to kick off.

"All right, guys," Saher says. "You've all been chosen to be here because of your different skills. We've got real client briefs for you to work on, which means your ideas have a possibility of being produced. My goal is to have you walk away from this experience with something you'll want to be known for."

The briefs build on the strategies of two existing AMV clients. First is Mercedes, who hope to add more excitement to their brand, which is known for luxury and class. The second is EDF Energy, a utility that wishes to continue distinguishing itself from the commoditized energy category through friendliness. With this brief, the teams are encouraged to consider utilizing the Zingy character, a tiny orange mascot made of just eyes and a nose on a body shape not unlike the poop emoji. Given that the poop emoji is the most popular emoji in the UK, it's no wonder Zingy is so loved here.

To me, a hackathon beats the typical unpaid internship by miles because, by striving for a working prototype in a short time, these young people will end up with an artifact they can use to demonstrate their thinking in future job interviews, as opposed to having only anecdotes from hours spent listening to conference calls. Not to mention that Forge has fronted the travel and housing costs for these talented teams in London. It makes me wish these events existed when I was starting out.

"Time pressure is a magical psychological motivator, as I'm sure you've all experienced in your own life," Saher says. "So each day will have a defined goal. Today's goal is nailing down an idea. Get familiar with your team, your brief, and let's get started."

To make sure that the teams leave with that tangible, portfolio-worthy piece or project, Saher draws a clear beginning and a clear end for each day of the hackathon. Day One is dedicated to locking down the idea. Day Two is all about scoping the idea. On Day Three, the teams will develop and start building. On Day Four, they'll finish building and practice their presentations. And on Day Five, they'll present to a group of AMV's senior management. (See *Recipe for a Hackathon*)

Saher has asked me to support him by floating among all the teams, just as he will be, building on their ideas and challenging their thinking.

With the teams already assigned, the clock begins ticking, and everyone hustles into their respective war rooms.

BEST VS. FIRST

The next morning, Saher and I bundle up and walk a serpentine path through quiet London streets and across a cobblestone square. It's February, so it's cold, but the sun is out and there's no wind. We reach St. Katherine's docks, where yachts that I'm sure would rather be cruising through the Caribbean are berthed. Just past the yachts, we approach a little café being run out of a mini-truck. The Italian barista has made Saher's double macchiato without sugar before he's even ordered.

The last few minutes of the walk take us through a tunnel that spits us out in front of the medieval Tower of London, and for a moment, I feel swept back in time.

I see Saher juxtaposed with the historical icons, flicking through his iPhone as we board our train. Inventor and engineer Charles Kettering once quipped, "We should all be concerned about the future because we will have to spend the rest of our lives there." Saher seems to embody this advice with a constant concern for the future.

"Your chapter is going to be a little shorter than the others if you spend these two weeks on your phone," I tease him. Saher is the youngest sibling in his family and I am the oldest, and this dynamic has manifested itself in our interactions.

"I was just getting a head start on the day," he says. "The groups sent some of their ideas across last night."

He reads them aloud, and we discuss their merit as the train bumps and veers around the dark tunnels of central London. We exit at Marylebone and walk toward the office. Our breath visible, Saher and I discuss what feedback we'll give the teams. We agree that the ideas fall into two camps: those that would create new products and those that would be considered campaigns, creating interest in the brand. Neither is "wrong," but for our purposes, to create something in such a short time, we are focused on the campaign angle.

The distinction between products and campaigns for me is the two different goals. When creating a product, it's important to be the best. In this instance, the path moves from minimal viable product to beta test and then through iteration after iteration to the final polished, joy-delivering experience. If you're a social network like Facebook or a delivery service like TaskRabbit, you want to be best. These companies weren't the first to hang a shingle and go into business in their respective categories, but they persevered with a customer-centric view of providing value while turning a profit.

With campaigns, on the other hand, it's more important to be first. If you're finding a way to produce a pizza box that can be transformed into a movie projector that works with your iPhone (as Pizza Hut experimented with in Hong Kong), there will be significantly less good juju for your brand if Apple has already launched the very same idea with their cardboard phone packaging.

"Why don't you spend the morning with the Mercedes team?" Saher suggests as he opens AMV's front door for me.

The Mercedes team has come up with an idea to create a test-drive app for salespeople to use with customers: The app would give the test-driver feedback by quantitatively measuring biometrics, like heart rate, and report just how much the customer's body has reacted to their test drive. It's a fun idea for Mercedes, and, done well, could easily give the brand some tech cachet.

PROTOTYPING WITH TRAINING WHEELS

Chris, a muscular former Swedish Marine turned producer, attempts to clear some of the clutter from the team's war room. Soda cans and Post-it notes abound. Manning the whiteboard is Boris, an English user-experience designer whose hairstyle has him constantly pushing a curtain of fringe to the side. As I pull my notebook out of my bag, Ina, a slim, Lithuanian innovation designer, picks up a whiteboard pen. Sam, the mobile developer, and Albin, the Finnish programmer, both slump in their chairs. They look like they slept in their clothes even though we're not to the programming stage yet.

The team's whiteboard is full of scribbles and arrows that make less sense than the quick e-mail summary of their idea. Some elements even stretch into mad scientist territory. It's wishful thinking, at least for now, that an app could read someone's thoughts. The team walks me through all their thinking, and we begin to dissect the ideas, sorting the realistic from the fantastical, the powerful from the weak.

"Before building this thing for real, let's take an intermediate step," I say. "Saher suggested we use a prototyping tool to flesh out the idea."

Advertising agencies are no strangers to prototypes. The humble mock-up of a press ad and the well-worn storyboard script are both, technically, prototypes.

But the expectation in business today is that new ideas should expect far less from our imaginations, especially when we're evaluating ideas involving technology. Or perhaps it's the lack of experience with technology among marketers that necessitates prototyping.

The tool Saher recommended we use is an app called Prototype on Paper that will let us make a mock-up prototype of the Mercedes app idea before putting in all the effort of coding a working prototype. In mere minutes, the team is on to the next step of negotiating which features ought to be in their app.

"From the test driver's perspective," Boris says, "we need enough feedback to prove that the ride was exciting. But neither the salesperson nor the driver should be touching the app during the drive."

It warms my heart to hear them putting themselves in the user's shoes. As this is their project, I don't throw my own ideas into the mix but just chime in with "that's cool" or "I like that" to give them a boost as they align on the features. Having programmers Sam and Albin in the room is critical; we all turn to them whenever the inevitable "Can that be done?" is spoken.

Prototype on Paper is ridiculously simple to use. Boris is an artist and quickly draws each app-screen the team has imagined on sheets of paper. Then Sam takes a picture of each page while the rest of us look over his shoulder. With the pictures captured in the phone, he uses the Prototype on Paper app to select each picture and the areas on each that will be "hot" for a user to make a choice. Then the team must choose the next page where the link will take the user. In the process, small problems arise and they make decisions in the moment to add, tweak, or cut options and features. The finished prototype gives the illusion of a real app, asking the user to sync a wearable device and enter which car they're testing, and producing a dashboard readout after driving.

"What if we offer to e-mail the output to the user at the end?" Ina asks.

The group likes this idea and adds it to the now neat and focused list of features on the whiteboard. The prototyping exercise has been a success.

AN URBAN RAMBLE

After only a few days together, the projects are well under way. In a move to both reward and help gel the teams further, Saher has planned to host a party at his flat on Saturday night. "Trust is one of the most important components of a good team. You have to get to know each other on a basic human level to work well together," he told me.

We make a trip to the nearby Marks & Spencer, and I push the trolley while Saher loads it up with beer, wine, liquor, and snacks. The two liters of vodka tells me someone will surely puke tonight.

 At the appointed hour, the guests begin to arrive, and a mound of trainers and boots slowly builds in the front hallway. We all gather in the kitchen, making drinks and snapping photos and Vines. The flying fuck is very popular. I can see friendships forming, especially between teammates who didn't know each other before. No one pukes.

On Sunday morning, after Saher and I fill our bellies with lattes, eggs, and toast, he suggests we take a nice walk. It's a gorgeous sunny day and even warmer than it was during the week. We make our way back toward the Tower of London and across Tower Bridge. Amid the historical architecture, great swaths of tourists are taking selfies and group shots in the sun. We wander westward.

Rachel Hatton, a strategist with a wealth of experience at some of London's top agencies, did a talk encouraging strategists to walk more. It gets the blood moving, obviously, but also, she insists, getting up out of our desks can help us have more ideas.

Science backs her up. Our creativity tends to flow more freely when doing a task where the mind is allowed to wander, whether that's doodling, showering, or walking. In addition, simply being in contact with nature and the outdoors can boost creativity. Hatton also described walking as a radical act. Most protests are marked by marches: The sheer act of moving is diametrically opposed to our more common working posture of always sitting behind a screen. The thinking is bound to be different simply from this context.

Personally, I find that most men are more comfortable talking when they are side by side with their conversation partner, whether that's driving, flying, or walking, so I take this opportunity to ask Saher some questions about our first week together.

"I feel like a lot of marketing clients have what I'd call a pathological reluctance toward adopting new technologies." I say. "I've seen so many good ideas go unproduced. But this week I've spent with you has me wondering, if I'd pushed a little further toward making prototypes in the past, would any of those concepts have been produced?"

"What I've observed over the years," Saher says, "is that most marketing clients are under incredible pressure. They have budgets to account for and crazy deadlines to meet, so it's hard to be imaginative under those conditions. Even if they're highly imaginative and entrepreneurial, they're often trapped in the systems of their organizations. It's hard to innovate and take a risk on something that has never been done before. Lots of barriers come in the way: Whose budget is it? What's the ROI on an innovation project? Who owns the process?"

The gravel path that lines the Thames crunches underfoot.

"Having said all that," he continues, "maybe you're right: Maybe a prototype would have helped. But I think the majority of the time, working with a marketing team is a recipe for frustration. Instead, I've tried to instigate relationships with CEOs and managing directors to bypass the system. Most unicorns in the tech industry like Uber or Airbnb were born outside of the industries they revolutionized, so why wouldn't we learn from that?"

"Easier said than done," I say, remembering the many ideas I've seen die at the hands of CMOs and marketing directors before any CEO has even had the chance to know of their existence.

"The magic language is money," Saher says. "When the cost of failure is cheaper than the cost of analysis, making many ideas is a means of research. If you can get a client to see this, budgets begin to appear."

THE PROOF IS IN THE DOING

In the final days of the hackathon, the teams finish programming and testing their prototypes. They use every last minute to tweak and practice their presentations. At the appointed time for the reveal, everyone looks a little weary, but excited to show off what they've accomplished. The shared space of Forge has been transformed: Rows of chairs have been placed facing a makeshift stage, and all the team rooms have been stripped of empty Red Bull cans and Post-it notes.

"Are you ready?" I ask Sam, one of the programmers on the Mercedes team.

"I wish we had one more week on this!" he responds. "The worst was finding bugs at 2:30 this morning."

Saher approaches the front of the room.

"I don't shave that often," he begins, "but when I do, I use a handmade straight razor, the kind you'd expect the barber to use in the Wild West. Why do I like to do this? Well, there's the ritual of lathering up with the right soap, and the care it takes to shave properly. At first I thought of it as the male version of applying makeup. Then I realized it's also about looking after myself. The face is the most visible aspect of one's self. So using this tool, as opposed to a disposable razor, is a way of treating my face with respect. It's an attitude that if you're going to do something, do it well. That's craft.

"And that is what you are going to see today. Twenty young people have applied themselves, their craft, in a compressed time frame. Each team has a working prototype to demonstrate. There is an honesty in producing a prototype as opposed to describing an idea. There is a craftsman's pride."

Next, Saher introduces the teams and the briefs. The Mercedes team presents second. Ina and Boris expertly demonstrate how their app would collect data from a wristband worn by the customer test-driving a car. At the end of the drive, the salesperson can then reveal to the potential customer just how exhilarating the ride was by showing them the raise in their own heart rate and amount of G-forces they experienced.

In the audience, heads nod with approval. Ina and Boris are beaming.

After all of the presentations, Saher and I wait outside AMV for a hackney carriage—the omnipresent iconic London taxi—that he requested on his Hailo app. The car pulls up moments later, and we slide in.

"The Albion café in Shoreditch, please," he tells the driver.

"Right, sir," the driver replies.

I pout because he didn't call Saher "guvnor."

The Albion is a typical hipster café with clean Scandinavian design, an open kitchen, and lots of light. It's also the home of the first Baker Tweet box, a little device that, with the push of one button, lets a baker send a tweet notifying followers the moment fresh-baked goods emerge from the oven. This lunch marks the end of the hackathon, and it feels good to sink into our seats and relax.

As we chat, Saher mentions that he first took this job at AMV because he believes "we have to move at the speed of technology or technology will eat us. I'm obsessed with the idea that speed is good."

It's difficult to buy a "dumb" phone these days. Smartphones epitomize the changing technology landscape, and in response our social norms shift too: Today we tend to look at people who don't participate in some social media with distrust. The only constant is change, and I can see that Saher's strong point of view comes from a career of witnessing such acceleration.

After we order and make a few cursory comments about the presentations and the work still to be done of sharing the ideas with clients, I ask Saher, "I'm curious. What keeps you pushing the advertising industry from the inside when it so clearly does not move at the speed of technology?"

"Good question. The way I see it, technology is ahead of the consumer, the consumer is ahead of brands, and brands are ahead of agencies. But if agencies want to shake up that order, they have to bring these forward-thinking ideas in as added value. Brands need to know they can partner with their agencies to innovate. Everyone, I think, is realizing that we have to fundamentally un-learn what we've always done. We need to create new relationships. And creating something new where success isn't guaranteed is incredibly exciting.

"Plus the way I've set up my role, we're using the hackathon format to speed up processes and I get so much satisfaction from teaching younger people. Hackathons let me bring both the teaching world and the business world together. I enjoy the intense focus it brings: It quickly weeds out any inefficiency and any redundant thinking or doing. It sharpens everyone's instincts on getting the right idea and then getting the idea right."

"But that still doesn't explain why you're doing this in an ad agency," I say. "I mean, it's awesome that AMV is even willing to invest in a group like Forge when so many other shops aren't."

"I once met a Buddhist monk at a conference who was talking about sustainability. He really hated that word, 'sustainability,' because it implies reversing time and going back to the past, which you can never do. His belief was that we have to find a new way and think toward the future. We have to evolve and adapt. And I think that's the most important thing the agency world and the business world could possibly focus on. I have a lot of talent that the agency world can benefit from. I want to see it transform."

"You have the heart of an artist and the mind of an engineer," I tell him. "Did you ever see that comment that Kurt Vonnegut made about there needing to be a Secretary of the Future as one of the president's advisors? I think you'd make a good one. Really. The most important thing I've learned on this trip is that in meetings, we can talk or we can *make*. Our future depends on which one we lean toward most."

collaborative INNOVATION

BY SAHER SIDHOM

Before this latest wave of change took over, one could argue that an apt model of the organization is a sandwich. It's neat, self-contained, discrete, and stand-alone. But given the onslaught of change, the enterprise today has to function in a more open way. So much so that it's often hard to distinguish where it begins and ends. The whole economy has become more like a plate of spaghetti.

Companies can no longer afford to think of a linear value chain that they alone control. Instead, the emphasis shifts toward ecosystems of value.

A phone manufacturer fifteen years ago used to be concerned only with developing physical phones. Today, making the hardware isn't enough. Apple and Android have built ecosystems for external developers to build on their platforms. Even Apple and Google with all their might couldn't have built the billions of apps now in their stores. Microsoft, too, once regarded as an arrogant bully, is learning to collaborate and woo developers with Visual Studio, a code editor that can write apps for Windows, OSX, and Linux. Technology forces us to collaborate and open up.

Yochai Benkler, professor of Entrepreneurial Studies at Harvard and author of *The Wealth of Networks,* sums this up elegantly: "The world is becoming too fast, too complex, and too networked for any company to have all the answers inside."

A friend of mine just launched a start-up that provides a wonderful app to estate agents in Berlin. He couldn't have built his company without tapping into the API that provides the properties he features. By building on the work of others, new value is created. In short, I submit to you that you cannot spell capitalism without "API."

recipe for a
HACKATHON

BY SAHER SIDHOM

Years ago, I was a part of a start-up that was failing miserably, and so we decided to dissolve it. We met with an Italian guy who specializes in buying failing companies. He buys them, splits them apart, and sells the pieces. After he bought us, I learnt an important lesson from him, because he came in and literally took the chair from underneath me.

When I objected to the removal of the chair, he very calmly said to me, "*Verba Volant, Scripta Manant*," which is Latin and means "Words fly, what's written stays." Our contract had not specified what happened to our office furniture, and his point was if it wasn't in the contract, we weren't getting it.

Since then, I've hated contracts because they're usually designed to divide and punish in case of failure. Years later, I decided to write my own contracts in order to do the opposite: to ensure people know their contributions are protected and more important that they'll get a fair share of collective success. This way, people are motivated to contribute their best ideas rather than holding back. But it has to be codified, like a recipe. With the right and fair basis for the engagement, a psychological commitment develops where success depends on how well we collaborate instead of on how well we fight over a share of the idea.

The current advertising agency business model doesn't account for retaining intellectual property (IP). The current model is designed to sell time and to give away ideas. Once we present an idea to a client, the client owns the idea, which is absolutely not motivating to teams trying to make the next great thing. If an idea can transform a business, or at least create value for the business, the agency should have a stake in the IP.

fall down every

RABBIT HOLE

BRIAN MILLAR
Sense Worldwide | London

chapter NINE

"Woo the muse of the odd."

– Lafcadio Hearn

Two For Joy is my favorite coffee spot in Amsterdam. Don't misunderstand. I really do mean coffee. You'll be disappointed if you go expecting the other kind of coffee shop. (For that, I'd recommend Happy Feelings.) The skylights at Two For Joy make you feel like there might actually be a wide-open blue thing up where the big gray masses of cloud usually sit.

I cradle my cappuccino, watching my laptop screen and waiting for a Skype call from Brian Millar, director of strategy for the innovation company, Sense Worldwide. Brian was a total stranger when I first approached him for this project. I'd read one of his articles on Fast.Co about researching atypical people in the service of innovation and knew I had to at least try to work with him.

I'm very keen to spend time in an innovation consultancy. Having read about IDEO and met a few people here and there who work in innovation, I'd always suspected the work is somehow more fun. But given that almost all of the work is project based, I wonder just how involved strategists would be in bringing ideas to life. Luckily, a shared connection was willing to introduce me to Brian.

At noon sharp, my laptop screen lights up with his incoming call.

"Hi, Brian," I say, adjusting my earbuds. I'm a little nervous.

"Hi, Heather," he responds with a friendly smile.

Over e-mail, Brian was receptive to the project, at least in theory, but I still had to persuade him to commit.

"I was so intrigued by your article," I say. "You have to tell me what it's like to interview a dominatrix. I've met one here in Amsterdam, but it never occurred to me to bring her to work!"

"Ha, well, yes. It made me really appreciate the relaxed dress code we enjoy here at Sense."

Brian has a kind manner, which loosens me up. I explain my project to him, and emphasize that other people have already agreed to participate. (I can't be *that* crazy.) Then I go in for the kill: "I'm not trying to be paid while I work with you, but the thing is, I've been staying in the homes of my hosts. Do you think your family would be up for that?"

We stare at each other for a moment.

"Yeaaah," he nods slowly. "I think this could be fun for us. We have people stay with us quite a bit, so Samira and the kids are used to it."

I can't believe he's going for this!

"So you let me know when you get back from Asia, and then we can plan a good time to come to London," he says. "We'll just make sure there are some good projects on."

THE HOGWARTS OF STRATEGY

Several months later, I'm back in London. I dodge the tourists shopping on Oxford Street, turn right on Wardour Street, and drag my suitcase to number 68, the global headquarters of Sense Worldwide, the self-proclaimed Hogwarts of Strategy.

Rather than running through a magical wall full-tilt to get in, I must instead pull my suitcase up two flights of narrow, steep stairs and open the door to the birch-colored offices of Sense. An Australian woman, Kirsten, greets me and calls Brian to come down—thankfully—from the floor above to meet me.

"So wonderful to finally meet you in person!" I say when Brian comes through the double doors.

"Welcome to Sense, Heather!" He's equally enthusiastic, and I'm introduced to his signature 1,000-watt smile. Brian is tall and lean with a mop of thick, gray hair. He looks rather sporty in jeans, a Nike zip-top, and trainers.

After we've tucked my suitcase into the coat closet, Brian gives me the grand tour. Sense operates from the top three floors of this building. The first two are studio space full of desks, books, magazines, whiteboards, and temporary foam-core panels leaning against the walls and covered in rainbows of Post-its. The top floor reveals an incredible loft space set up like a living room and used for the many workshops they conduct.

We take a seat in the loft to chat about the two weeks ahead. As I admire the view across the rooftops of central London, I expect the chimney sweeps from *Mary Poppins* to emerge at any moment.

"There's a great project we're just starting for the Cabinet Office that should give you a good feel for the type of work we do," Brian says.

The Cabinet Office is a department of the UK government whose civil servants are responsible for many programs fostering the social good.

Brian leans back on the couch across from me, stretching his arms outward. "The government is concerned with the alarming level of online fraud against Britons, things like identity theft and phishing scams. Part of their concern stems from the amount of money lost, but the bigger problem is sort of under the surface. If people don't feel confident online, Britain's economic growth could be at risk. Did you know that the top two Internet passwords are 'password' and '123456'?" He chuckles. "And most people do not keep their antivirus software up to date unless they've experienced a problem in the past.

"The Cabinet Office has done some interesting work to make people think about their privacy. They made a microsite called The Devil's in Your Details that scrapes your publicly shared information from Facebook and then presents a short film of a stalker who appears to be stalking you. It's really creepy and makes you think about all the things someone with bad intentions might be able to learn about you."

"Wow, that is creepy. This sounds like a fantastic project," I say, giddy to dive deeper.

With just over twenty people, Sense feels more like an extended family than a megacorp, but Brian's role in that family is more eccentric uncle than patriarch. He might be a director, but he's also the guy who's comfortable wearing spandex cycling kit on his regular hour-plus commute from New Malden (you've got to be a bit mad to ride a bike in London traffic), and he's also able to draw on quite an eclectic career. In his past, he's ping-ponged his way across an array of experiences from reading English literature at Oxford to copywriting and creative directing in top ad agencies, to brand consulting on his own and writing compelling articles for business publications, all before his current post at Sense.

Luckily, Brian has switched from cycling to riding the train for the two weeks of my visit, though this switch actually complicates his commute. At the end of my first day, he proceeds to lead us both on a dizzying transfer from work to home. First, we shove my suitcase into a taxi from Soho and take a ride to Waterloo Station. Then, we hop on the commuter rail southbound to New Malden. We finish with a walk from the train stop bringing us to the Millars' Tudor-style home, which is positively palatial compared to London apartment living.

"So nice to meet you, Heather!" Samira, Brian's wife, says as she emerges from the kitchen into the foyer. They call for Arun, thirteen, and Lakshmi, eleven, and make introductions. After I've settled in, and Arun has finished his violin practice, Samira gathers us all in the kitchen for a perfect roast-chicken dinner. The conversation shifts effortlessly from the typical tales of the day to funny online memes.

As a presenter for the BBC, Samira is hyperaware of current events: "I spent most of the day discussing this elitist Cabinet minister scandal," she tells us.

A British official was accused of calling a police officer a plebe when the officer asked him not to walk his bicycle through the main gate, although the official insisted he didn't say it. "Plebe" isn't a word I often hear, and for me the news is a reminder of the classist undercurrents of British culture.

Brian and Samira got together at the end of university just before landing jobs. With lots of free time, they fell in love while watching daytime matinees. Their home is bursting with books, fit into bookshelves like a game of Tetris all throughout the house. And "palatial" is perhaps too diminutive a word to describe their home. It seems to magically expand as you go up the stairs or around corners, just like the adjacent possible. It was Samira's childhood home, but her parents haven't strayed too far. They now live a few doors down the road, further evidence that it takes a village to raise a family when both parents work.

ELUSIVE INNOVATION

The next morning, Brian and I commute back into the city, joining the other suburban Britons who are wrapped in scarves and coats, clutching coffees and handrails.

"Tell me about the kind of clients that come to Sense," I say.

"Well, we're into what we call transformational innovation. Meaning if you're merely looking for incremental growth and sustaining innovations, then Sense is not the right partner to work with."

Clients such as Nike, Converse, SC Johnson, Vodafone, General Electric, and Diageo, to name but a few, have chosen to work with Sense because they appreciate this refusal to deal in mild, step-change innovation; they're in search of a more elusive innovation, one of the especially disruptive variety.

In 2014, Ernst & Young did a study called Delivering Agile Innovation, which analyzed innovation practices in corporations. They discovered that 53 percent of packaged-goods companies and retailers rely on outside innovation help. The very culture and processes needed to take burgeoning business ideas from back of the napkin to profitable multinational products often hinder future innovation; it's hard to innovate from inside the machine. Even Google has split their most creative, sci-fi, semi-secret R&D into a separate entity: Google X.

McKinsey also studied corporate innovation and found that in 2010 most global executives admitted to struggles: They reported that while 84 percent of executives worldwide think that innovation is an important part of growth, only 6 percent are satisfied with their innovation performance.

Still, why should mighty corporations suffer public failures by rolling the dice themselves? Due to the intense financial pressure many of them are under, they tend to adhere to the philosophy of simply looking for smaller emerging companies that demonstrate promise, and then acquiring them along with their respective brands. This philosophy helps them to avoid the messy 70 percent failure rate that new products must hurdle, but it doesn't mean they won't drive their newly acquired companies into the ground. Quaker, for example, nearly destroyed the Snapple brand it purchased for $1.7 billion, selling it for a paltry $300 million just three years later.

While mergers and acquisitions are one strategy for growth, most businesses must face the hard slog of coming up with new ideas and *then* making them operational. There's a palpable fear among the executives I meet in Hyper Island classes that their companies may become the next Blockbuster or Nokia. They know they need to innovate, but all humans struggle with change; those in older companies are no different. "Innovation," business icon Peter Drucker has said, "is the specific instrument of entrepreneurship . . . the act that endows resources with a new capacity to create wealth."

If innovation is an instrument, Sense is both a guild of artisanal instrument craftsmen and a bevy of child prodigy performers. *Innovate or die* has become one of today's most common business mantras, ensuring a significant pool of potential clients for Sense.

"Clients come to us wanting to transform, wanting to do something different," Brian tells me. "Nobody has an R&D department big enough anymore. It's also been interesting to discover that companies can be sitting on business models or products that just need a tweak to find their place in the world. Flickr started as a feature within a video game. Hermes started out making saddles. Kleenex was brought to market as the first disposable cold cream towel."

"Wow, I didn't know that. So with the anti-fraud project, where do we begin?"

"You've really got here at the perfect time because we're just kicking it off."

We arrive at Waterloo, and I mind the gap as I exit the train. We head upstream through the many commuters.

"The first thing we do," Brian says, "is what we call a Research Amnesty. Most companies have hundreds of thousands of pounds worth of research, if not more, sitting on an intranet. And since it's online, they know that no one looks at it. Well, that's the first place we investigate. We pore over all of the research that no one has bothered to read and pull out what's interesting, which leads to sharp questions for further research."

I love this idea of a Research Amnesty. Sure, I've been a part of many a discovery process that involves conducting research audits, but there's something about a catchy name to make the act more credible, and to hopefully encourage the clients to turn over all the research they have instead of sharing only what they feel is relevant.

Brian steers us toward our morning coffee at a little red shop front in Soho. The curved red awning reads "Algerian Coffee Stores Ltd Est 1887." We go inside, order lattes, and then browse the shelves as we wait. They're chockablock with canisters of beans, stove-top espresso makers, and confections. The quick service has us back on our way in no time, and we walk the last block to the office.

A COLLECTION OF HUMANS

Dr. Faye Miller from the TV show *Mad Men* is an early prototype of today's strategist. In a memorable scene from season four, she gathers the young, single office women into the boardroom to psychoanalyze their purchases of cold cream. Don Draper, the creative director, wants to make cold cream part of a beauty ritual, so Dr. Faye probes for any evidence of its habitual usage among the ladies. Instead of proof of Don's strategy, the talk of beauty soon derails toward unrequited love, and one secretary leaves the room in tears.

After the "focus group," Dr. Faye and Don Draper have a go at each other over their interpretations of what they've learned. Dr. Faye reports that all the women want husbands, and so a smart strategy would be to link the product to the promise of a husband. Don counters that it doesn't matter what these ladies think right now, because if his campaign runs for a year, *his idea* is what they will believe in the end. "You can't tell how people are going to behave based on how they have behaved," he tells her.

I learn that Sense and Don Draper hold similar beliefs about research when Brian takes me to a Japanese spot called Bone Daddies for lunch, where we discuss Sense's philosophy toward research while eating steaming bowls of ramen.

"If you think about typical research," he says, "most of it seeks out the mainstream to validate ideas. Regular people make up the bulk of the population, the big meaty middle of a bell curve. You go out and talk to them year after year and they rarely tell you anything new. So, for example, if you talk to runners you get the same kind of information about losing motivation to run when the weather is bad. But what's really interesting is if you go and talk to extreme ultramarathon runners, because the world isn't designed for them. They have to hack their shoes and clothes to make them work for their needs."

This practice of seeking out and investigating such people was the topic of Brian's Fast.Co article on extreme users, which is where I first learned about Sense. It's what really sets the company apart.

I had scoured books on innovation in preparation for my visit, and found that IDEO's Tom Kelley briefly mentions the practice of searching the fringes of consumer behavior in his book *The Art of Innovation*:

> *Just as we often can't predict a product's success, companies can't always divine what feature or use will catch the public's imagination. For that reason, companies need to be in touch with what "quirky" uses consumers have thought up for their products, and be ready to restructure their marketing accordingly.*

Eric von Hippel, professor of Technological Innovation at MIT, was also interested in people who significantly modify currently available products to meet their niche needs, naming them "lead users." Sense, too, deliberately sniffs out these "quirky" uses and hacks. This might mean talking with a guy who constructed a homemade flamethrower from a bicycle brake, a lighter, and an aerosol can to kill bugs, or touring the refrigerator of a Mormon whose bigger family may just mean different refrigeration needs.

Sense has gradually built up an extensive global network of creative and imaginative people in what they call the Sense Network. They can take polls and gather early intelligence, or tap into their collection of humans to find other, more relevant people for each new project at hand, and so these interviews compound in value over time.

With the fraud-prevention project, we plan to pursue all sorts of leads. For example, I'm already scheduled to interview a reformed hacker who goes by nothing more than the handle "Cruzer," and there's an interview scheduled with an entrepreneur in the privacy space whose business is trying to introduce image-based passwords, where users must touch four points on an image they've uploaded instead of attempting to concoct and remember secure text passwords.

Brian, perched on his stool, slurps up a noodle and then begins waxing philosophical about the method of working with extreme users. "By bringing these sorts of voices into big companies, you get inspiration rather than validation. We often bring these people into our workshops. They suggest ideas right alongside us and the clients. That's really powerful."

"Not your typical crowdsourcing, huh?" I say.

"Exactly. Most people don't have anything creative to say. Using their suggestions just leads to mediocre designs and communication. Besides, it's interesting and entertaining to meet exceptional, creative people. These are the people already living in a possible future, so the validation is baked in.

"Now it seems strange to only talk to regular people. What if they only tell you what you already know?"

JOBS TO BE DONE

Toward the end of my first week, Brian and I are in a conference room with Jacky Parsons, Sense's research director, going through some of the things we've learned from the Research Amnesty on our laptops. Blonder than me and far wiser, Jacky shares a framework I haven't seen before: jobs-to-be-done theory. It was created by Clayton Christensen, best known as a Harvard professor who specializes in innovation and the author of *The Innovator's Dilemma*.

"In jobs-to-be-done theory," Jacky says, "you take the perspective that everything we buy, whether a product or a service, is being hired to do certain jobs for us. And those jobs are often not the jobs you might expect."

Christensen came up with the theory while working on a project for McDonald's in the US. In an effort to sell more milkshakes, McDonald's R&D explored all sorts of flavors and bits to create more interest in their milkshakes. But each test market showed that these innovations had absolutely no impact on sales.

Enter Christensen. His team began by observing the McDonald's customers who bought milkshakes. They could see from sales data that there were a few spikes each day when sales were highest, but they were most interested in the early morning spike. Who buys milkshakes at 8:00 a.m.?

By speaking to several customers, they discovered that these milkshakes were purchased by customers making long, boring commutes to work. The milkshake staved off boredom, because it took about twenty minutes to consume. It was also highly portable, without risk of making a mess. Perfect for the car.

When you look at innovation through this lens, the potential competitive set is far broader than just smoothies and other milkshakes.

"Christensen believes that we hire products and services to fulfill functional, emotional, and social needs," Jacky says.

The idea begins to sink in, and I realize something like an audiobook, instead of a milkshake, could be hired to counteract the issue of boredom, thus satisfying the emotional need to distract oneself. A yogurt could substitute for the functional need for nourishment. It's only through interviewing different people who use the product that the real jobs products are hired to do are revealed.

Jacky turns her laptop so Brian and I can see a slide. She points at the screen, which shows two arrows pointing right above two arrows pointing left. "Christensen believes that any switching moment is driven by four forces. There's the push of the situation, as in a person having a job that needs doing. And there's the pull of a new solution: We can be magnetically drawn to something by sheer novelty or because of the magnetism of the brand. Those two forces encourage a switch in behavior. But then there are two forces that keep people from switching: There's the anxiety that a new solution won't really get the job done, and there's the habit of doing whatever you've been doing. Basically, inertia. Think about these four forces in relation to changing our Internet passwords."

"So if my password is one-two-three-four-five-six," Brian says, "I'm really unlikely to change it, because of habit. I don't have any anxiety about just using my old password, because I've never experienced anything bad, nor have I heard of others openly talking about negative consequences. Nothing is pulling or pushing me to change."

"You're jumping ahead," I say. "That's exactly what we've found in the reports from the Research Amnesty. People aren't concerned with changing passwords unless something bad has happened to them, and by then it's too late. And it's not just habit and inertia pulling them. Many people think they don't really have anything to steal."

"So we've got to create an awareness that there actually *is* a job that needs doing," Jacky says, "or we've got to establish that there's a reason to be anxious about maintaining the status quo, or we've got to devise some way of looking at passwords that's so novel everyone will want to take part. The model isn't rocket science, but I think it's a helpful tool for looking at the problem."

"Really nice," Brian says. "What I like about this is that it helps articulate the problem in human terms. Fraud isn't a problem for most people, but there's no job to be done if that's the starting point."

THE QUEST FOR A RICHER LIFE

Brian and I take a day away from Sense to attend Playful, a conference of sorts covering topics from the world of games—everything from board games to video games. I especially enjoy learning how to play the Danish Clapping Game. (Google it; it's good fun.) While most strategists would love to attend such an odd little conference, most companies would frown on having an employee spend a work-day indulging his curiosity when there's no toy or video-game client to apply any learning toward.

That everyone I've spent time with for this project is a curious person goes without saying, but Brian seeks experiences beyond his busy family life and interests on a regular basis just to see what he might learn. He's stayed an extra day in São Paulo at the end of a business trip, for example, and visited the museum of African history where he learned that Brazil held slaves far later than most nations. When he had to drive from Chicago to Milwaukee, he purposely took local roads and stopped anywhere that looked interesting, including a gun shop that sells deer urine and a salvage diver shop whose owner has trained billionaires how to dive for possible treasure.

To me, his way of being epitomizes Ian Leslie's view of curious people, which Leslie explains in his book *Curious* in this way:

> *Life would be more straight-forward if we knew what we needed to find out, if we were told at birth exactly what we need to know to be happy. But in a complex world, it's impossible to know what might be useful in the future. Curious people try things out and allow themselves to become productively distracted. They know that something they learn by chance today may well come in use tomorrow or spark a new way of thinking about an entirely different problem.*

We're spoiled for choice when it comes to good coffee in London, and Brian takes me to another spot, just two blocks from the office in Soho, called Bar Italia. It feels like a small piece of Italian real estate has up and moved north as a respite from the busyness of central London. It's a cool day but not cold, so, since we have scarves and jackets on, we take a small table in front of the café. The sky is threatening rain, but we're not worried as the tables are under an awning.

"So, have you always had so many diverse interests?" I ask. "I mean, the interest in cycling beyond simply getting from A to B, the endless reading, the countries you've traveled to, just saying 'yes' to things like Playful without an immediate reason to go? Most people are too busy with their work to live this way."

"Good question," Brian says, "Yes, I think I've always been like that." He takes a sip of his coffee, thinking for a moment. "My dad's a scientist and—I now realize—a fantastic explainer. Our house was always full of magazines and computers he brought home from work. So it's always been entertaining for me to follow lines of idle curiosity for fun, long before Wikipedia made it so easy. Most of the really creative people I know are always making odd links between different disciplines. My most recent rabbit hole has been finding out how an octopus might think, as it has nine brains."

"But I think you put in more effort than most people," I tell him. "This isn't just your hobby. Your days are full of work, commuting, helping to take care of the kids. You should be more tired, not investigating how an octopus thinks!"

"I suppose it comes from a worldview that goes something like this: As a human, you're in this amazingly privileged position of being in a bit of the universe where, for some reason, a load of atoms have coalesced into something that can actually observe the rest of the universe and think about it. You only get a certain amount of time to do that, so it seems a waste not to."

Zen transformed through curiosity. I'd join that church.

I've mentioned before that one of the most common clichés amongst strategists is to describe ourselves as curious. *Of course* you have to be curious to be a human in order to learn, but the thing is, as we humans get older, we do tend to let ourselves get comfortable. It takes vigilant effort to stay curious. And it's just this sort of vigilant effort that Brian demonstrates, and that I find inspiring. He's created a vast foundation of knowledge to make his creative work easier.

Benjamin Jones, a strategy professor at the Kellogg School of Management, has investigated the age at which Nobel laureates made their breakthrough discoveries. Before 1905, the average age was thirty-six. After 1985, that average jumped to forty-six. His rationale for such a jump stems from foundational knowledge: "If one wants to stand on the shoulders of giants, then one must first climb the giant's back. As knowledge accumulates, the harder this climb can become."

Harder for the obvious reason that there is more knowledge to obtain, but also because in our current culture, Google can provide an answer in .0004 seconds, and Netflix's algorithm can predict everything we will enjoy watching. If we're not careful, we might never stumble upon productive distractions ever again.

"What's your take on Google's algorithm and the like reducing our chances of stumbling on new things?" I ask.

"Well, I grew up in a small town where, if you wanted to stumble on something new, the only place to go was the library . . . which was great for large print romance novels but not much else," he says with a laugh. "I can't imagine going back and living that way. I do think the Internet is a fabulous place to be for the idly curious."

Brian is more than "idly curious" in my estimation, and as such, his willingness to follow his curiosities has morphed into a creative superpower. But it's the effort he puts into falling down rabbit holes, not the resulting creativity, that is the virtue to emulate.

TRYING ON A LIFE

"I got my first computer at age twelve," Cruzer tells me over Skype.

We're not using video and he's not sharing his real name, because he's broken the law in the past and wants to remain anonymous. I detect an eastern European accent, but I can't discern anything else about him.

"My father was in the military," he continues, "and he saw computers and got one for our family. When I first saw it, I thought it was a UFO. But I played with it, got to know it, broke it, fixed it. That's when I fell in love with technology."

"How did you become a hacker?" I ask.

"At that time, Internet security was flimsy. One of my connections from World of Warcraft had insider information about an Austrian telco company. He'd some stolen codes that let him break into and take over anyone's phone that had the Bluetooth switched on. Together, we made a program that would access these open phones, make a phone call to the US, and then hang up, and that one call would charge the person ninety-nine cents. I would hang out in airports and train stations to troll for the right kinds of phones. I made crazy money doing this. Something like five hundred thousand euros."

"Wow. That is crazy," I say. "Was that the only time you did something like that?"

"No, I've done so many things. I think the one I'm most proud of was when I broke into this yachting website. It only had three hundred members, so I figured they must be rich. I got in and found one guy's info, started poking around in his credit card statement, and found out he was into really devious porn. So, to punish him, I ordered two hundred blow-up dolls to be delivered to his house."

"Ah, so you're a vigilante hacker!" I say, laughing. "What would you advise regular people on how to protect themselves . . . people who don't know much about computers, who are just using their e-mail and Facebook. How do they protect themselves from people like you?"

"People in general are ignorant. For them, ignorance is bliss. But if I were giving advice . . . number one, get a Mac or install Mac OS on your computer. Then install Little Snitch, so you know if someone is trying to get into your computer. And then, just learn by example. I'd show you what people can do on the computer to make you vulnerable, like how clicking on a bad link can give someone access to all your contacts. To me, technology is a form of evolution. It's weeding out the stupid people."

"You mentioned to my colleague that you've stopped hacking," I say. "Why is that?"

"Well, I got into it at a time when the top three dreams of young people are to be a footballer, a singer, or a hacker, right? And a hacker is different from a cracker. A cracker is someone trying to get passwords to make a mess with e-mails; a hacker is someone who wants to prove themselves. We're motivated by challenge. We want to beat ourselves. It's like getting a new high score on a game. But after a few years of it, I had so much money and I started developing vices. I wasn't the kind of person I wanted to be. So now I'm a web developer."

"If you were working for the government, any government, what should they do to stop hackers?"

"Where do I even start?" he says. "Governments could do a lot to set standards. You know that little padlock logo that tells someone a site is secure, right? Businesses should be regulated so that their sites are really secure. The government could issue companies official holograms for their sites to prove they're authentic just like we have on currency. The tech exists, but businesses aren't compelled to use it."

It's fascinating to step into such a different life from my own. Cruzer's story could easily be the plot of a movie, and it helped me to visualize a more vivid picture of what we would be protecting Britons online from, rather than just the Nigerian spam I've typically come across. My chewing mind kept pondering how the government might paternalistically steer behavior among citizens, and how we might motivate behavior change so that citizens do what's necessary to protect themselves.

BEHAVIOR CHANGE

Magda Lechowicz, a Sense consultant, and I have been working together closely, poring through every research document like detectives trying to piece together evidence from a crime. In fact, we could make a great season of *True Detective* together, playing a tall, blonde, female crime-fighting duo.

We've curated the CliffsNotes of our Research Amnesty by pulling out the key points and crafting the previously hidden story that the many research reports tell, and put this all up on the wall by Magda's desk. We further build the story with salient points from the extreme interviews with people like Cruzer as well as in-home and on-site interviews with citizens and business owners.

On Wednesday afternoon, we're joined by Jacky and Brian to walk them through what we've learned so far.

"I think this model will help us frame the task when we share these findings with the client," Jacky says as she adds BJ Fogg's Behavior Model to the wall. "It says that a behavior happens when a person has sufficient motivation, ability, and a trigger. They must all be present at the same time for a behavior to occur."

For example, think about being asked to sign up for an e-newsletter that offers knitting patterns for dog sweaters. Entering your e-mail address in a text box is very easy, but unless you actually have a penchant for Chihuahua jumpers, you'll never give up your address, no matter how many times you are asked.

On the other hand, it is possible to do something very difficult if there's enough motivation. Running a marathon, filing a tax return, or attending a physics lecture all require significant time, physical capacity, and mental capacity (all aspects of ability), but with enough motivation and reminders, people do these things every day.

"Well then," Brian says, "we really have our work cut out for us, because all of the research we have says Britons lack the motivation, ability, and triggers to change their behavior proactively."

The research shows, no real surprise, that changing a password is perceived as a huge hassle. Sufficiently safe passwords are difficult to remember, and multiple passwords compound this problem. Apps such as 1Password and Dashlane have emerged to solve this challenge by creating and remembering secure passwords, and Facebook Connect allows a user to log in to an external site with his often already cached Facebook username and password, reducing entry to a site down to one click. These solutions are all ways of simplifying the behavior of logging in to a site.

Any behavior becomes easier to do when it costs less, takes less time, requires less physical or mental capacity, and doesn't feel socially deviant (like wearing a bathrobe to a dinner party would feel). A behavior is more likely when we can tap into core human motivators such as belonging, aspiration, and pleasure (or avoid the opposite: the human demotivators such as rejection, fear, and pain). It's safe to say that the average Briton's motivation to change his password is nonexistent, but to protect his reputation? We found that, universally, people tend to untag themselves from unflattering Facebook pictures and avoid asking questions they feel would make them appear to be a n00b. We began to wonder if we could connect safe online behavior with protecting one's reputation.

Britons expect to be compensated for any online fraud or hacking; therefore, they don't worry about losing money. But reputation loss? That particular toothpaste doesn't go back in the tube. Our discussion about avoiding embarrassment with a few simple steps got our interview participants to lean forward in their seats, while talking about potentially losing money did not.

As Brian, Jacky, Magda, and I hashed out a plan for our upcoming workshop with the Cabinet Office, we all sensed we'd be bringing them some thinking they'd not previously considered.

DOING IT WRONG

Stephen King, who I mentioned in Chapter 7 and who was one of the founding thinkers in bringing brand strategy into the advertising agency, also happened to lead the team that invented the Mr. Kipling brand of cakes. Funny thing is, J. Walter Thompson was initially briefed to sell more flour. Their solution was to create a brand of prepared cakes—Mr. Kipling—which, by necessity, require flour. While there are many ideas coming out of agencies today that don't count as "typical advertising," creating an entirely new brand from scratch is not a commonly observed solution.

In my experience, execs in ad agencies love to dabble in innovation. We're idea people who can't be reined in to merely communicating about a brand. But few of the ideas that stray from direct communication ever see the light of day. I must admit, I'm still a little bitter that the lapkin—a napkin large enough to tuck into the seatbelt for in-car eating—didn't capture Burger King's imagination. The idea emerged only after we'd spent several weeks ideating new innovations . . . but perhaps it was just too horrifying for the clients to see what American food culture has become.

I had another experience working on an innovation project for StrawberryFrog that showed me my advertising skills are applicable beyond communications. Our client was Kraft's Philadelphia Cream Cheese, and their R&D team had developed a liquid form of the cheese that could just as easily be whipped into a dessert as stirred into a soup or stir-fry. While it had been flavored and presented as a sauce in the US, the question for our team was what would be the best way to go to market in Europe?

We interviewed a cheese historian—yes, such a person exists—and then conducted a workshop with chefs who specialized in the three leading markets' cuisines: English, German, and Italian. By inviting the chefs to play and experiment, we hoped we might discover what role the cheese could serve in these very different food cultures. We were especially interested in any commonalities that might show up. Afterward, we explored the semiotics of different packaging choices: For example, we thought a pouch might keep the product the freshest, but it turned out that in some countries this is the packaging of choice for wet dog food.

The project culminated in a fifty-page report. About *cheese*. And it was fascinating. Advertising, it was clear, was no longer just about advertising. It was at this moment, holding the final report in my hands, that something occurred to me: If I could spend all this time helping to dissect the possibilities of a new cheese product, my identity as "working in advertising" was too narrow. But there are so few opportunities to stretch our abilities beyond advertising if we're working in advertising agencies. No matter how much we all talk of change, agile consultancies like Sense are diving in headfirst while most agencies are only toe-dipping.

On my last evening in London, Brian takes me to the members club at the British Academy of Film and Television Arts. We sit in tall wingback chairs, sipping cocktails.

"I still don't know what I'll do next," I tell him. "I've loved aspects of every job I've seen at Sense, and aspects of every job I've ever had. I know no job is perfect, but all jobs are limiting."

Brian sips his drink. "Time spent as a strategist or creative in ad agencies trains you to do a whole lot more than the role requires," he says. "It's a beautiful combination of rationality and instinct. But it's restrictive. I can't imagine going back in."

This reminds me of one of the articles he's written for Admap where he said directly to us strategists, "If you're still doing it in an agency, you're doing it wrong."

"I think what's interesting about Sense," I say, "is that you're all specialists in generalism. You all seem to easily snap back to beginner's mind with each project. Do you agree?"

"Hmmm." He thinks for a moment. "I think there are 'hedgehog' people out there who know a lot about a little, and they tend to have a very rigid model of how their area of specialism works. But being eclectic makes you a perpetual outsider—in a good way—because you're able to take a different perspective and ask stupider questions. Like Darwin, who was a geologist before he was a naturalist. Or Pope Julius II, who asked a sculptor to paint his chapel ceiling. The biggest breakthroughs in twentieth century economics came from two psychologists (Tversky and Kahneman) and two mathematicians (von Neumann and Nash). Advertising used to attract more of those 'square pegs.' I hope innovation does now." (See *Strategists Wanted*)

Paul Buchheit, creator and lead developer of Gmail, also warns us of the seductive dangers of experience in his 2014 commencement speech at the Startup School Europe:

> *We already know better, we already know that an idea or business won't work. This is one reason that naïve, young founders are often the ones who start the most successful companies–they just don't know any better, and they're often too arrogant to listen to those who do.*

As I close this chapter of both the book and my life, I hope I can hold on to this feeling of the wide-eyed explorer, of not knowing better, of knowing teachers are all around me in many forms. No matter where I go next, I'm grateful for the experiences I've had, and I know I need to remain unattached to the idea of "right" and "wrong" ways of working. The challenge is to keep pulling ourselves toward the next new idea, braiding and bending our experiences and amassed knowledge into beautiful, unexpected new forms.

STRATEGISTS wanted   BY BRIAN MILLAR

If you're reading Heather's book, you're probably a smart strategy person, so it shouldn't be too hard for you to take the Clayton Christensen jobs-to-be-done model and apply it to yourself. What are you being hired to do by clients?

Don't be modest. What you do is unique. You have the creative ability to make a big, disruptive leap for the client's business, and the numeracy to make a watertight case to the board for why they should invest in it. Think how uncommon that is. A designer can do one bit, but is rarely credible in front of the CFO. A McKinsey partner will only go as far as the data lets her–she won't commit to doing something entirely new, where there's no best practice case study.

But you can, you clever little left-brained right-brained thing, you.

Right now, you're being prevented from doing that job. Because you're being used to justify the hunches of creative teams and sell ads or digital marketing or media space even when they may not be the best solution. There's a simple reason for that: You're connected to a big factory, and you have to sell what that factory makes, even if it's in a classy, consultative way.

It's the job an ad agency has hired you to do, not what a client really needs you to do.

Few people can make a $1 billion call on an idea. Even in Hollywood, those people are rare, earn millions of dollars a year and have sex with movie stars. Advertising is full of planners smart enough to do that, yet dumb enough not to reap the rewards.

Advertising has had a great run, but when I look at the emergent innovation industry, I see something akin to Madison Avenue in the 1960s: a convergence of real talent, a refreshing lack of rules, and from our clients, a massive appetite for new ideas. Design companies, research companies, big consultancies, and small specialist shops are converging to form an industry. It's an exciting thing to help to build. You should take a look. There are some big jobs to be done over here.

CONCLUSION

**"You have to learn the rules of the game.
And then you have to play better than anyone else."**
– Albert Einstein

"You are remembered for the rules you break."
– Douglas MacArthur

"I'm really jealous of what you're doing."
– Everyone I met while researching this book

Nine coaches. Six countries. The passport is covered in stamps, and the project is over. So much has happened in two short years since I began. Rachel Adams, Phil's wife, passed away unexpectedly. rOobin discovered he had a brain tumor the size of a tennis ball, named it Ivan, and successfully had it removed. Rob lost his amazing mum to rare complications in surgery.

Thankfully, it wasn't just sorrow that visited after I left. Jason and Meredith welcomed Millie and Dash's new sister, Twyla, to their clan and traded Hong Kong for Paris. Rob and his wife Jill introduced their son Otis to the world. Kevin and his wife Christine became US citizens. Eventually, Suzanne left CP+B and joined McCann. Simon started an additional consultancy, Kepios, alongside his We Are Social role. And Saher left AMV BBDO to start his own tech-and-design research studio, HACKMASTERS.

I don't think I could have ever predicted just how wonderful it is to have my life intertwined with the lives of these beautiful people.

When I began this project, I deliberately focused on my work life, hoping that the rest of my life would simply sort itself out. I assumed I would want a full-time job in the end. I assumed I would choose where to land based on an affinity for a particular city I'd visited. I assumed there would be many opportunities in Asia. I assumed that while cruising along on my other assumptions, I might meet some guy and move country for him.

I did meet some guy, but he was in Amsterdam and, in the end, he was willing to move to follow me.

I hunted for new types of companies where I could apply my skills. I listened to Brian's advice carefully: "If you're doing it in an ad agency, you're doing it wrong." That advice conflated with a rising complaint I was hearing among many of my peers: Is there any place to work where it's still fun anymore? And my inner wisdom told me: The advertising agency business model is struggling.

So I surprised myself when I returned to CP+B to work for Suzanne, which also meant a return to Miami.

WE'RE ONLY GIVEN AS MUCH AS WE CAN HANDLE

While on my adventures for this project, I'd maintained a home base in Amsterdam, and every time I returned there I'd get together with my former boss from StrawberryFrog Amsterdam, Melinda Eskell. It was partly because Mel had struggled to find a job after leaving StrawberryFrog herself that I took the job in Miami. I thought that if Mel couldn't find work in Amsterdam, as incredible as she is, I had little hope.

Mel had been the managing director at StrawberryFrog, and we'd gotten on very well for the year and a half we worked together, but it was after we'd left our jobs there that she began regularly inviting me to her home for dinner parties, and we became even closer friends over coffees. When I wasn't off gallivanting on these book trips, I would freelance from Amsterdam, and she was always a wise sounding board for me on any difficult project. And she helped me launch the Amsterdam chapter of House of Genius (houseofgenius.org: Look it up, you'll love it).

Not only was Mel there to help with my work life, but she became someone I could turn to for advice about my personal life too. She was supportive when I started falling in love with a man thirteen years younger than me, even when other friends weren't as understanding (turns out he was some *young* guy). She invited Aaron—my guy—and me over for Christmas dinner, and then for Easter. When I accepted the job with Suzanne, she celebrated my new gig and my rushed-for-visa-reasons marriage. When she then landed a great new job herself, we celebrated again, this time over e-mail.

My point is that while I was busy looking around the four corners of the earth for mentors, the best mentor relationship I could hope for was developing in my own backyard. The same could be said about love. I was busy looking out in the wide world, but he was in my neighborhood bike shop all along.

Then I woke up one June morning, in some airport hotel in Milwaukee, where I'd been attending some focus groups, and discovered via Facebook that Mel had passed away suddenly and unexpectedly.

The tears are coming in fast now even as I remember this moment. Just when I'd found someone who took an interest, who saw me as a precious jewel, who was willing to invest time in me for the long haul, she left me.

My inner critic knows that this is an incredibly self-centered thing to think. The loss for her family and her friends of many more years is far, far greater. But in such a short time, I had learned so much from her. I felt cheated. I wanted more time. I wanted happy reunions for twenty or thirty more years.

So this is the first of five lessons I learned and that I will leave you with: You don't have to travel around the world looking for mentors. There is probably someone superb nearby . . . someone whom you already know.

In interviewing each of my coaches, I learned so much because of the shared living arrangement that encouraged them to share not only their work life with me but their personal life as well. This helped me realize I'd never connected with any previous bosses as deeply as I did with Mel. I'd never put in the same effort to know the other people I'd worked with: my potential mentors. The massive amount of work to be done always seemed to be the more urgent demand on our attention and energy.

But now I realize that when we are too consumed by our work, we miss out on truly knowing each other—on sharing our experiences and mental models. We need to make more time to share.

The second lesson? If you do discover someone willing to invest in you, treat her as the prized jewel that she is. Don't just expect her to treasure you. Work hard to find her, but work harder to keep her. You can count on not having her forever.

THAT LEARNY FEELING

Even though my best mentor was so close to home, traveling around the world looking for mentors *did* transform me in positive ways. My skills as a strategist grew exponentially as I traveled, and I learned so many unexpected lessons. I learned how to best approach the beginning of a project, how to recognize the power of my own empathy, and how to search for Zen. I learned to push myself to care even more, and to be comfortable with exploring the fringe of digital marketing. I learned how to design brands that lead culture, how to investigate new consulting models, and how to work hard as a maker. And above all, I learned how to embrace my curiosities.

I also learned that mentors aren't always in human form: Pangs of jealousy can also be teachers. They give us clear signals as to where we should steer our energy, and they point us toward our genuine selves. They reveal which goals we should aim for.

It follows that you should be jealous of this project. If you're a strategist worth your paycheck, you love learning new things and the sense of the unfamiliar—of tasting a new idea for the first time. I made the familiar suddenly unfamiliar with travel and through meeting new people.

Sociologist Benjamin Barber boils it down like this: "I don't divide the world into the weak and the strong, or the successes and the failures . . . I divide the world into the learners and nonlearners." Psychologist Carol Dweck, who researches achievement and success, went further in her book *Mindset*. She identifies the fundamental mind-set difference between nonlearners and learners: Nonlearners believe that their intelligence and talents are fixed, whereas learners believe intelligence and talents can be grown over a lifetime. If we can't do something, it's not a sign of insufficiency; rather, it's an invitation to try something new, to learn, to grow.

It's all too clear to me that while companies benefit most from people with growth mind-sets, few are interested in helping us find ourselves or training us. Phil helped me to see this in a positive light when he wrote on his blog: "Goodbye jobs for life. Goodbye logical, linear progression. Goodbye security. Hello handbrake turns and hiatuses. Hello work-as-adventure if you have the right attitude and the right level of self-awareness."

This project was just such an adventure. A life prototype.

The third lesson for me demands that I hang on to that feeling and avoid getting too comfortable. As Leo Tolstoy said, "Everyone thinks of changing the world, but no one thinks of changing himself." I now know that mastery is a constant pursuit, and that while jobs are one place to learn through experience, personal projects allow the complete control that leads to mastery. Always having a project that stretches our skills, like this one did for me, keeps our antennae tuned to new ways of thinking and working, while refreshing the skills we've already amassed.

A NEW WAY TO LIVE

Finding career bliss is tricky.

On this journey, I learned big things. And small things. I confirmed what I already knew: I still have a lot to learn. I scared the shit out of myself realizing I'll never know everything, or even half of everything. Because the cheese is always moving. And I learned that I like doing lots of different things. I'm an aspiring polymath, and most strategists I've met are too.

When I decided to leave CP+B for the second time, I spoke with Saher, who at the time was in the midst of leaving AMV and setting up HACKMASTERS. "I'm not prepared to let my talent die trying to make an ad agency look cool," he told me. Whether in the UK or the US, large agencies tend to attract painfully slow-paced clients who struggle to green-light forward-thinking ideas. Saher isn't willing to waste his time and now, after less than a year in business, HACKMASTERS already has the majority stake in two intellectual properties and nine clients who are gung ho about bringing ideas into the world. Clients like this are out there.

Doing brilliant work is important to me. But so is working in a way that isn't all consuming.

I'm not ready to start a business on my own—the reasons why would take up a whole other chapter—but I do know I have a lot to offer. Even while finishing this book, I've been flexing my muscles as a freelancer and teaching more classes with Hyper Island. I've done projects that have stretched my skills and taken me all over the world. I've taken courses in improv and stand-up, and I'm now certified to teach yoga (what?!). Most important, I've had time to spend with my hot, young husband.

Do you remember Mr. Wolf from *Pulp Fiction*? He comes in to quickly and efficiently help Jimmie, Vincent, and Jules get rid of a body. At my best, I'm the Mr. Wolf of strategy, and it's a role I hope to develop further. So if you find yourself in a strategic pickle, give me a call.

The fourth lesson I've taken from this experience is that freelancing or owning your own consultancy while still having a life is a valid aspiration for all of us to reach for as strategists. While there aren't many people openly modeling this choice, there are a few. A prime example is Genius Steals, a consultancy with no office. Founders Faris and Rosie Yakob live on the move. Willem van der Horst, Strategist Survey team member, has also worked as a nomad, making time for scuba diving and home brewing. And Heidi Hackemer, founder of Wolf & Wilhelmine, purposefully designed her business around taking breaks so that she and her team can feed their inspiration. This small sample proves you can be both an excellent strategist and a vivacious human.

PUTTING OUR INGENUITY TO GOOD USE

As I wrote and wrote and revised and revised, Brian Millar took a course at the Faber Academy, an esteemed creative writing program in London, and began writing his first novel. We swapped writing techniques and inspirational essays by writers who have gone before us, and he prompted me to think deeply about the crux of this book as he read early drafts and offered feedback: "The reader will want to know why somebody with a life that most people dream about—living in one of the world's coolest cities, with an amazing job in an aspirational industry, whose apartment is listed on Foursquare as a karaoke bar—decides to question it in a really profound way, and throw it all up in the air. And why she doesn't go to an ashram, but heads out to talk to a bunch of advertising people."

My response, dear reader, stems from my (perhaps strange) belief that life is a lot like performing a circus plate-spinning act. For me, there are three plates: career, city, and love. And each plate has a question: What to do? Where to live? Who to love? (Maybe you have a "kids" and "health" plate, too, if you're a particularly ambitious plate spinner.) You might be able to keep a couple of plates going at once, but more? That's quite a feat.

So we make choices. We languish in a city we hate because of an amazing job or for the love of our life. Or, alternatively, we turn down a work opportunity to stay in our city. Or we drop everything and follow love.

I've never mastered spinning all the plates at once. Maybe I'm especially hard to please, restless even. I took on this project knowing I was completely open to a new city, a new job, and to love. I simply had the idea to apprentice myself, decided it was a good one, and went for it.

But it was the commitment I made to write a book that took me on the greater adventure. Despite knowing intellectually that brands must be created for the long term, my living in a project-based world for so many years has created an imbalance in me toward short-term thinking. And while a book can be broken down into smaller tasks, it is a long-term, integrated construction unlike any brand work I've ever worked on. Both agency and client, in my experience, have a bias toward short-term results, and that's to our detriment.

I don't have a ready solution, but I suspect it's to be found in creating a brand of my own. Not just a service business that only scales with more people, but a branded product built with growth in mind. Noah Brier, a former strategist who went out and founded his own company Percolate, hinted at this when he told me, "I really enjoyed my time in advertising. That's where I learned the power and value of brands. But I taught myself how to code because I wanted to make things. I'm not sure why strategists aren't thinking in products. I like writing my own destiny."

There is no resource more precious than time. Being decisive has served me well in making the most of mine. But just as I was finishing the book, I went to study yoga for a month, allowing me to ponder my use of time. I watched the film *Samsara*, a powerful visual and music mash-up of nature, cities, and the diversity of humanity. Scenes of volcanoes were juxtaposed with shots of slums and slaughterhouses. I learned about ecopsychology, the study of the relationship between human beings and our natural world. We all know that we're running the planet down; the question becomes, what do we, in the context of our working lives, do about it?

We have powerful problem-solving skills. Jason Clay, VP with the World Wildlife Fund, gave a stirring TED talk where he revealed that approximately 80 percent of the world's commodities are controlled by only one hundred companies. If those resources were sourced sustainably, we would be well on our way to tackling the fact that we already need 1.5 planets to support the current world population (which is only growing). You, as strategists, get time in front of the CEOs of these companies. Each brand has the opportunity to lead culture. Every meeting you have with a client is an opportunity to change things.

Dan Price, CEO of Gravity Payments, provides another example of a corporation leading culture through their policies. He made a bold announcement to raise the minimum salary to $70K for all of his 120 employees. He chose to do this after reading of the significant impact income up to about $70K per year has on happiness. After only a couple of months at their new salary, employees already reported having savings, paying down debt, and helping family members financially. This new income freed them from their personal worries and woes, and they discovered they could instead focus their energy on making Gravity Payments great.

I found this example profoundly touching. More and more companies like Toms and Patagonia have based their business models on sustainability and are doing well by doing good, but Gravity Payments' story proves that every company can play a role in making the world better. The workplace is in need of an overhaul to make it more human and I can't wait to see how we strategists help redesign it.

Otherwise, perhaps we all join Anonymous and take the baddies down, à la *Mr. Robot*.

The last lesson for me is this: We have more responsibility on our shoulders than I think we realize. We have skills that could save the world. We know culture. We know business. We have what Henri Poincaré called *aesthetic sensibility*, or the ability of the unconscious mind to know when it's stumbled on an insight interesting enough to pass on to the conscious mind. Whether we are advising companies or creating our own, let's use our unique skills to shake up the old systems and make change that matters.

about
the

AUTHOR

HEATHER LeFEVRE

Heather LeFevre is a modern marketer who earned her stripes working as a brand and communications strategist. After completing a masters degree in communications, Heather landed her first job at the height of the dot com bust, and from that point forward she's made it her mission to guide clients through the complex opportunities technology has made possible for business.

She served as Group Strategy Director at Crispin Porter + Bogusky's Miami office, where campaigns such as "Whopper Virgins" led to eighteen quarters of positive growth for Burger King. While Head of Strategy at StrawberryFrog Amsterdam, Heather led a comprehensive brand relaunch for Emirates Airline, one of the fastest-growing airlines on the planet.

Heather is currently a thought leader tapped by Hyper Island to teach master classes on growth hacking for executives all over the world. She lives in Miami, Florida.

@hklefevre
heatherlefevre.com

9 780996 854603